DA
235

THE CRAFT OF COMEDY

THE CRAFT

OF

COMEDY

by

ATHENE SEYLER

and

STEPHEN HAGGARD

THEATRE ARTS BOOKS   **NEW YORK**

Note

At the moment when the first specimen pages of this book were sent to me by the English publishers came the news of Stephen Haggard's death in active service in Egypt on February 25, 1943.

The joy and interest we had shared in this correspondence are now most poignantly clouded for me. But his enthusiasm and youth, the vivid quality of his mind, and the grace of his spirit shine in these letters; and I am glad to be able to send them out as a true remembrance of him.

Athene Seyler.

Introduction to the Second Edition

by Athene Seyler

It is now fourteen years since this little book first appeared and I am so happy that it has proved of use to students and also to others interested in the theatre. I have myself learnt more about comedy during this time and may perhaps allow myself now, in a new edition, the luxury of a few generalizations.

Firstly and lastly I am more than ever convinced of the health-giving properties of laughter. It is, in its best form, a kind of spiritual antiseptic, and I have noted again and again how it breaks up poison in people's minds and acts as a mental tonic; how it preserves balance in emotional crises and generally tones up sagging attitudes of mind. Believing this to be true I still take the greatest pleasure in practising the art of creating laughter in the theatre and have lately had some interesting experiences.

There are, it seems to me, technically two kinds of

comedy: one that lies in the witty line, and the other that is in the situation or the characters. For the first, only clear delivery of the author's words is necessary—and how lucky is the actor to have such a light task, for the really witty line is a rare thing. For the second means of ensuring laughter there is only one essential as I have tried to show in my letters—namely truth. The actor must feel deeply the circumstance, or his own point of view or emotion, and he must do this in the round as it were. There will lie hidden wells of laughter springing up in unexpected places if he follows fully his reaction and expresses the characteristic response to the scene in which he is playing, and often these comedic moments are unforseen by author and player.

Take, for example, a simple phrase like "Oh, really." This can be said in tones of fear, irony, mirth, horror, embarrassment, incredulity, and even in two of them at once. Now, if the actor is true to his response to situations and his own character and that of the other people in the scene, amusing light can be shed by those two innocuous words.

Another thing I have recently had proved to me is the power of an audience to show the actors what they had not themselves seen in a situation. An example of this is my own experience in the play in which I am at the moment performing. In one scene where I have a house-party I have been fortifying myself in an awkward situation with a glass or two of whiskey. This makes me stumble twice over the word "croquet" which

I first pronounce "coqret" and then "croqret." A few moments after this incident my son asks me where the guests are—the audience knows they are playing croquet. At rehearsal this question was put in merely to bring the son into the scene, and my reply to it was considered so unimportant that the author suggested I should simply say "Still playing." When I said this simple sentence on the first night, it got a sustained roar of laughter to everyone's astonishment on the stage. The reason, of course, was that I was apparently avoiding saying the word "croquet" again. The audience remembered my dilemma over it and the author and actor had overlooked it. This is only one example of the power of the theatre to create such a vivid impression on an audience that it actually illuminates the players and author.

Above all, some technical points have been impressed on me since playing for three years in theatres which have been too large for the plays we have performed in them. This has entailed first and foremost clear speaking—not shouting, but enunciating, with particular attention to the last word of every sentence. There is always a key word in a line, and if this is lost the whole meaning of the sentence (and in comedy, therefore, the laugh) is lost too. Often this key word is the final one of the line, and a fatal fault is to exhaust one's breath at the beginning of the sentence and let the final word become inaudible. The cure, of course, is to control the diaphragm so that the breath is conserved. But this properly belongs to voice production and is necessary for all acting.

Another essential technical detail is the generous giving of what we professionals call the "feed line." So often an actor thinks that the unimportant words he has to say to someone can be thrown away, when actually the reply is senseless if they have not been heard. Many otherwise thoughtful and generous actors are guilty of this fault without realizing it. When I have lost a laugh in a long run I always hold a post mortem on the scene, thus: Have I been heard? Have I been true to the sense of the line and character? Has the feed line been heard? —in that order.

Finally, to simplify and generalize, the secret of comedy acting, after the play and one's part have been thoroughly studied, is to listen carefully and to speak clearly. This sounds too easy, but may I assure the reader that it is not. Sometimes amateurs fulfill these two conditions out of innocence and because they have not yet become conscious of finer shades of expression and possible tricks of presentation, and the success of an amateur production is often due to the two formulae I have suggested.

There is never an end to learning about this job of playing comedy; it is never possible to probe completely its depths and subtleties. But with Stephen Haggard's help I have attempted in the following pages to guide the student through some of the early stages.

1957

4

THE CRAFT OF COMEDY

Correspondence

between

ATHENE SEYLER ═══════════════

═══════════════ *and* STEPHEN HAGGARD

8th June 1939.

DEAR ATHENE,

Not long ago I had a conversation with you in which we discussed comedy in the theatre in most of its aspects. Some days later I went to see Schnitzler's *Wedding Morning* acted by the——Bank Amateur Dramatic Society of which a friend of mine is a member. After the performance I had a talk with my friend which inspired this letter to you. My friend played Anatol. I think you will agree that this is an extremely difficult part for a young Englishman to play. His performance left a lot to be desired. He lacked a sense of comedy and played rather as if the *Wedding Morning* were a "straight" play which only occasionally (and rather reprehensively) lapsed into comedy. I could see hundreds of things wrong with his performance. But when he asked me to help him to improve it for the second (and last) night I am ashamed to say that I was at a loss to help him. If I had allowed myself to criticize him my criticism would have been destructive only. I have not the technical knowledge, nor the experience of playing comedy which would have enabled me to offer him something constructive in the way of help. I therefore said very little, until I realized that his true desire was not so much to improve Anatol for one performance as to learn about comedy—all sorts of comedy—because he wants to leave his bank and go on to the stage.

My friend seemed so much in earnest about his intention that I have been wondering whether you could possibly spare the time to write a few letters on the subject of comedy for his benefit. Speaking more selfishly, I am conscious of my own weakness in playing comedy and I hope I may find out something of the principles which underlie it before handing on your letters to my friend, whose name, by the way, is an appropriate one for a pupil, namely William Eager.

I remember your saying once that comedy is "distorted truth." Straightforward truth I think I can recognize—in the theatre at any rate. But how to distort it for comedic purposes—as to that I have only a rather hazy idea. William, I suspect, has none at all. So won't you please help my eager friend to settle the problems which perplex him? I shall look forward to learning a good deal "on the side."

Yours ever,

STEPHEN.

My dear S.,

Your letter has had the effect of placing me as it were "at the tape," prancing to be off down the course riding my hobby-horse, to prove to you all my theories about the art of comedy acting. If I am able to help your young friend I shall be more than pleased.

To start with then, I should say that comedy is simply a point of view. It is a comment on life from outside, an observation on human nature. Would you agree with me that emotional acting of a serious part involves absorption in the character—identification with it, losing one's own self in another's? If so, you will understand me when I say that, on the other hand, comedy seems to be the standing outside a character or situation and pointing out one's delight in certain aspects of it. For this reason it demands the co-operation of another mind on which this observation is to be made—the audience, and is in essence the same as recounting a good story over the dining-table. It must have direct contact with the person to whom it is addressed, be it one's friend over the port or one's friends in the stalls and pit.

I hope this does not give you the impression that I take a low view of comedy as something to raise the "laughter of the injudicious," nor that you will confuse it with the vulgar wink across the footlights to establish good fellowship, or any of the perfectly legitimate tricks employed in the music-halls or revues to "get a joke across" as the saying is. This branch of comedic acting is a very great one, but I'm afraid I haven't any real knowledge of it or its technique. I am only able from experience to discuss the interpretation in a play of an author's comic invention.

When I talk of establishing direct contact with an audience I mean a subtle psychological bond, perhaps merely the subconscious acknowledgment that the intention of your job as a comedian is to point out something to an audience, and that the audience's reaction to this makes up an integral part of your job. You must create a delicate thread of understanding of the character you are portraying between yourself and your spectator, so that, in a way, you jointly throw light upon it. I wonder if this strikes you as rather shocking? It is so opposed as an idea to the modern theory of losing oneself in a part and leaving all thought of an audience out of one's mind—of desiring merely to re-live a set of circumstances and allowing the spectator to peep at them, as it were, unacknowledged. So that when I talk of a comedy point of view I find that I see this as a state of mind in which one desires urgently to point out one's delight in some aspect of a character to someone else.

Now if you were to ask me how to induce this point of view you would have me rather beat. Because I have to confess that I fear it cannot be induced, that it is a quality of mind which is either born in one or not. But in case this should sound too discouraging to your young friend I must modify my first reaction to the question and suggest to myself that it must be possible to acquire this quality. What does it imply? I shall shock you still further and suggest that it involves a light and superficial glance at life! Comedy, shall I say, is the sparkle on the water, not the depths beneath: the gay surface, the glint of sunlight—any other pretty metaphor. But note, the waters must run deep underneath. In other words, comedy must be founded on truth and on an understanding of the real value of a character before it can pick out the high-lights. It is only when one thoroughly understands a person that one can afford to laugh at him.

And here I would stipulate another quality that I find indispensable to the comic spirit—that of good nature. I am aware that this is a debatable point and that it may well be a personal idiosyncrasy of my own, but to me comedy is inextricably bound up with kindliness. As soon as a comment on character is inspired by contempt or anger it becomes tragic and loses the light of laughter. Irony, satire even, must be charitable and compassionate at heart or they stray into the realm of serious comment.

Can you apply any of this to your friend's performance of Anatol for a start? Was he regarding Anatol in the glancing light that heightened his character, or was he immersed in and perhaps swamped by his realization of the whole character? In that little play he should have picked out lightly certain gay frivolities and irresponsibilities about Anatol that adorned his deeper character. He should have slightly distorted one side of his nature—exaggerated the aspect of him that he wished to show us. For comedy is bound up with lack of proportion. It is technically dependent on accents of emphasis. It is not concerned with presenting a balanced whole: it consists in sharpening the angles of the complete character. Perhaps Mr. Eager had only got to the stage in studying Anatol of seeing him as a whole, and had not yet found the particular aspects of him that needed comment. Does this suggest anything to him, I wonder? Shall I say that comedy should upset the balance of a character and that he, perhaps, had only seen it in proportion to life, not slightly distorted.

This is only a rough suggestion of what I think may have been wrong with Mr. Eager's performance; and I await with some trepidation your own reactions to my idea of the principles which underlie the playing of comedy.

Yours ever,

ATHENE.

17th June 1939.

DEAR ATHENE,

Your extremely interesting and prompt reply leads me to hope that this correspondence may develop into a spirited epistolary bombardment; I only hope I shall be able, with scarcely more than a couple of unremarkable stage cannon for my defence, to hold my own against your accurate and quick-firing comedic guns. Perhaps I'd better take each shot as it comes.

Yes: I agree that emotional acting of a serious part involves losing oneself in the character, but I had not realized that comedy acting involved "standing outside" a character to the extent which you imply. I had imagined that this method was only right for farce, and that for comedy one should be as "lost" in the character as one is in tragedy, and that the very fact that one was so "lost," so convinced of the character, was what created laughter—provided that the character was in itself a humorous one. The comic characters of Chekhov— Epihodov in *The Cherry Orchard*, for instance—seem to me to need complete reality in their acting; any "standing outside" them would, I should have said, tend to destroy the spectator's belief in them and therefore his delight in their absurdity. On the other hand, I quite see that the method of complete sincerity cannot be right for the characters of, say, *The School for Scandal* or *The Importance of Being Earnest*.

I suppose the truth is that there are many different kinds of comedy acting, ranging from the unconscious humour of an Epihodov to the "conscious" humour of a George Robey, and that the art of acting comedy consists in choosing just the right balance between the conscious and the unconscious which each character demands.

I have little experience of acting comedy myself, but

I know from life the difference between causing laughter by relating something which is in itself amusing (comedy through situation), and so exaggerating the relation of some perfectly ordinary experience as to create laughter at the manner of telling it (comedy through character?).

Then, too, there is the comedy of being "out of character." On the few occasions when some frivolous remark of mine has made you laugh you have observed that the remark was "out of character." You consider me to be a serious-minded person and so the remark surprised you. Translated into terms of the stage this would be equivalent to leading the spectator "up the garden path:" he is keyed up to expect one thing and is suddenly presented with another. This sort of comedy could apply to both character and situation, I suppose, as in the case of the mock-conjurer who said he would produce a rabbit out of a hat and after searching in the hat apologized because he could only find a "hair."

No doubt there are many more nuances of comedy and I ought, if only as an exercise, to try and think of them all. But this I shall leave to you. One thing seems clear. All degrees of comedy have in common the "subtle psychological bond" by which you say one establishes contact with one's audience. This, I think, they share with all forms of acting. What is peculiar to comedy acting, however, is this distortion of which you spoke in your letter. You say that comedy aims at "upsetting the balance" of a character. But would not a comedy part be richer in performance if one *preserved* the balance of the character and, instead of picking out for emphasis "certain gay frivolities," related them to such deeper characteristics as were consistent with the author's invention? I do not see that the comedy would suffer as a result of this, any more than the last comic lines of *Juno and the Paycock* suffer from the tragedy that just precedes them.

Would it be presumptuous of me, Athene, to suggest that the choice of emphasis should rest rather with the author than the actor? And is one not being slightly unfaithful to an author if one singles out certain characteristics for special comment at the expense of others?

I realize, of course, that this (perhaps rather irritating) suggestion is all very well in an academic argument about comedy but that it completely disregards the personal—or perhaps I should say the personality—element in acting. That is something upon which you did not touch in your letter. I look forward to hearing what you have to say about it. I suspect that, in the last resort, comedy acting much more than straight acting is bound up with the actor's personality, and that it is the actor's personality which unconsciously chooses the bias he will put upon a part. This might explain too why you, who are so kind a person, insist that comedy should be inspired by only good-natured laughter, when for me, who am of a less generous nature, irony and especially satire may contain much that is bitter and yet not be tragic.

All this is by the way, however; what really matters

is whether William can make head or tail of it or not. I shall send your letter on to him and see what he says.

Yours ever,

STEPHEN.

30*th June* 1939.

DEAR STEPHEN,

Your letter makes me think twice if not three times! I must make myself a little clearer about "standing outside a character" in comedy acting.

Of course one must be lost in the personality one is playing, and when you say that the comic characters of Chekhov need complete reality you have only stated the fundamental law of all acting, comic or serious. Surely all artistic creation must be founded on truth; but one can regard truth from different angles, I should have said.

Should we not first agree on the basic principles of humour? Having done that we can then examine a part in the light of them; we can stand outside the character when studying it and measure the truth by the comedic principles. This sounds very solemn and is of course a clumsy attempt to analyse what every natural comedian does instinctively—but it may be valuable to try to lay down some rules.

What, then, is at the root of comedy? The essentials are: lack of balance, distortion, over-emphasis or under-emphasis, and surprise. Now, all these things are only relative to something else: the truth. So that you must first see the truth of a character before you can upset its balance. But you must *believe* in the distorted view of the truth that you have discovered. Having drawn the character a little out of proportion you must passionately believe in that measurement as the correct one. I think that your true comedian does both these things at once; that is to say, he is aware instinctively that the emphasis he is laying on one side of his portrait distorts it, and yet he offers it as a true likeness. The "standing outside"— the approach to the character—is the first process. The second process is concerned with presenting this view, and depends on what we call technique. It is the craft of appearing to believe in the balance of a thing that one knows is out of balance. This sounds like a theory of tight-rope walking! And indeed I think it is mental tight-rope walking, in which the slightest slip ends in disaster. If you forget the whole character while presenting one angle, or if you lose your vivid consciousness of this angle in your realization of the other sides of the character, your intention with regard to the audience will be lost.

To take Epihodov as an example: he illustrates the quality of humour that lies in over-statement. Every little misfortune that occurs to him he sees as a major tragedy. Now if you stand outside him his fears are ridiculous; you know that a spider can easily be brushed away, and that Epihodov will never use his revolver. But he himself magnifies a spider into a real menace and believes that he might one day kill himself. If you play the part from the inside (as he sees life and himself) it may well be a tragic performance of a man bordering on insanity. But if you are aware of him from outside as a foolish, impotent, harmless fellow all the comedy will be apparent. Of course there are situations where a comic character can appear either funny or pathetic, and sometimes, I believe, an audience can be divided in its reactions. I remember a very great comedian, James Welch, playing in a play called *The New Clown*. He was a little man who joined a circus because he was starving and, if I remember correctly, was not a real circus performer but tried to do the job without any training or knowledge. As the time of the performance drew near he was seized by panic, and the manager, fearing he would run away, locked him up in a small room. The audience saw the "clown" trying to escape from this room so as not to have to perform; and his growing fear and inability to tackle the situation, his final hysteria and suggestion that he would throw himself out of the window, kept the audience in a continuous roar of laughter. I saw the play many times—but, far from laughing, I always wanted to cry in that scene. James Welch used the comic effect of over-statement, for the situation was not as frightening or hopeless as he thought it. But he must have lost this outside knowledge for a few moments and allowed himself to believe in the character's own fears for me to have felt terror and pity instead of laughter. Now the actor should hold these two aspects of a part in his mind at once: he and the audience both share a secret from the character itself. If the actor is really frightened the audience will be frightened too; but if he knows subconsciously that his fear is out of proportion to the danger the audience will enjoy it.

(In passing, you say that perhaps the choice of emphasis in a part should rest with the author and not with the actor. But one knows that an actor can twist a serious character in a way which will cause laughter, or alternatively he may fail to amuse an audience in a part that is designed by the author to be funny. Therefore it is not quite so simple as leaving it to the author.)

I have tried to suggest the psychological background of comic acting as I see it, but the means by which the actor interprets the author's intention is another matter and is bound up with two things—personality and technique. Technique can be acquired. Personality, I suppose, cannot be altered. But I should hesitate to say that personality was a bar to playing comedy; it is only a help or a hindrance. Many great tragedians succeeded in comedy. Garrick was as fine a comedian as a tragedian. But Mrs. Siddons and Edmund Kean seem to have failed in comedy. Mantzius says that Mrs. Siddons had a preference for lively characters like Beatrice in *Much Ado About Nothing*—a preference by no means shared by her audiences! "The weight of her style, her seriousness, her lofty beauty all hindered rather than helped her lighter passages." Of Kean, Mantzius writes: "He seldom ventured on comic parts and never felt any great confidence in his powers in this line . . . now and again he would attempt one of the comic figures of the classical repertory, as, for example, Ben Jonson's delightful little tobacconist Abel Drugger, which had been one of Garrick's best comic characters. Many thought him excellent in this part, among others William Hazlitt . . . but he himself was not satisfied and only played the part three times. Garrick's widow wrote to him, after his first appearance in her husband's famous part, in the following laconic terms: 'Dear Sir, You cannot play Abel Drugger, Yours etc. Eva Garrick.' To which Kean replied no less laconically: 'Dear Madam, I know it. Yours etc. Edmund Kean.'"

So you see that personality may be a hindrance to playing comedy, even in the greatest actors. But, of course, both Kean and Mrs. Siddons were people of such outstanding personality that they may have been only the exceptions which prove the rule, and the very greatness of their qualities in one direction may have hampered them in the other.

My own belief is that an actor should be able to compass any part that falls within his *spiritual* comprehension, even if it is outside his physical equipment. There is one instance of an actor I know well personally who can suggest cruelty, tenderness, weakness, strength, stupidity and intelligence: but his one failure is in expressing coarseness. He may assume the externals of a coarse-minded man in his make-up, way of walking, clothes and manner, but his approach to the character is imposed from outside and he never succeeds in convincing the audience of its truth. So, in comedy, if your understanding of the humour of a character is lacking I am afraid no technical accomplishment will enable you to present it faithfully, though there should certainly be some comedy which will fall within your grasp.

Have you noticed that young people usually find comedy more difficult than serious parts? That is my experience as a teacher, except in cases of "born comedians," whom we need not consider, for they know instinctively the things which we are trying here to hammer out. Now why should inexperienced young people find it easier to lose themselves in the portrayal of a serious character than in a comic one? I think the answer is given in my theory of "standing outside" a part; for one needs "perspective" and a knowledge of human nature before one can place a character in a comic relation to life. One needs a large, tolerant and not too serious point of view—a view lacking necessarily in young folk, and lacking perhaps too in great geniuses of the type of Mrs. Siddons and Kean, who were superbly caught up in one torrent of expression, and limited by it. Personality is, after all, the external expression of one's mind and soul; and as these are moulded and enlarged by experience, so one's personality may well become more comprehensive until it includes a humorous side.

I had an interesting experience a few years ago of

working with an actor who had made a great impression in sinister parts. He essayed several comedy rôles during the time we played together; in one or two he was extremely successful, but he utterly failed in one light-comedy part. The successful performances were in the nature of caricatures: they were characters which he saw as laughing-stocks in real life. He was able to convey his sense of their stupidity and affectation in the true comic spirit. But when he tried to play a gay, light-hearted, charming, superficial character the mordant quality of his mind could not find anything to bite on, as it were, and the character escaped him. He did not understand it spiritually. This made his personality a complete bar to his successful playing of the part, in fact he relinquished it altogether.

So now, for the moment, have we disposed of the question of "personality." To sum up: I should say that it is a help or a hindrance inasmuch as it expresses outwardly the inner qualities of an actor, and if these are limited in understanding of the lighter aspects of life, so will his personality limit his powers of comic interpretation of them.

I am sure, however, that technique can help to overcome certain difficulties of personality, and in studying technique one can perhaps enlarge one's point of view and so acquire a more useful personality for comedy. I know of one actress, a serious beauty, who in her youth had no comedy vein, who has in later life acquired a great sense of comedy. And I suspect that this is a result of what she has learnt through enlarged experience both of life and of the technique of acting. This leads me to believe that if we try our hand at the technical craft of playing comedy we may in the process enlarge our own personality in a comedic direction.

This letter is getting too bulky for the post, so I will leave you here to send me your reactions.

ATHENE.

20th July 1939.

DEAR ATHENE,

You will see from the above date how hard and how long I, in my turn, have had to think about your letter.

I want to ask a lot of awkward questions.

First—(I have a feeling somebody has said this before)—what is truth? I mean, of course, truth in the theatre. Elusive though Truth is supposed to be, ought we not perhaps to pin her down with some sort of definition? Can one really regard her from different angles, as you suggest one should, or has she not perhaps a Victorian figure which can only properly be appreciated in the round? If you agree with Hamlet that the purpose of playing is to "hold a mirror up to nature" we have a very good yardstick with which to take her measurements. She must conform, brow, bust and bustle to what we are accustomed to expect from nature. An inch too much here or there and she changes her shape: we

23

no longer recognize her as truth. Of course a skilful dressmaker may clothe her so that she appears to be truth long after she has lost her figure. This doesn't matter so long as we still *believe* her to be the same. It is the skilful actor's job, I suppose, to make the audience believe. How he does it, whether by complete verisimilitude, or by forcing the audience with a succession of good-natured winks to "suspend their disbelief" makes no difference to success. Success will be his if the audience believes.

But what kind of success? Will it be the success the author intended? I think the answer is: not necessarily. As you yourself say, an actor can "twist a serious character in a way that will cause laughter;" and as this seems to me a very favourite trick on the stage I should like to put in a word for the author who, I submit, *does* know how his characters ought to be played and who ought therefore to be allowed to choose the emphasis to be put upon them. To go back to Epihodov: he is funny and not tragic because he himself never believes he will shoot himself any more than we do, and therefore he could be played from the "inside" and still be funny. The emphasis that an actor ought to put on the playing of this part is quite plainly indicated by the author and ought to make an approach to the part from the inside funnier, because more convincing, than the approach of an actor who plays him from the outside and therefore must rely principally on his own personal mannerisms to create amusement. Surely the "outside" approach ought to be restricted to farce, in which the author merely indicates certain general lines for a character and expects the actor to fill in the gaps with his own comic invention.

I understand you to suggest that until experience of life or some pleasant quirk of nature has given one a spiritual comprehension of humorous things one is unlikely to shine as a comedian in the theatre. But it does seem to me worth while in the meantime to perfect one's technical ability for playing comedy, so I am extremely interested in what you say lies at the root of comedy. The essentials, you say, are lack of balance, distortion, over-emphasis or under-emphasis and surprise.

What do you mean by lack of balance? Are you really referring to technique—to the *conveying* of a part—when you use this expression? Distortion presents no difficulties. One sees it every day in the newspapers. It is the art of convincing the public that the false is true. Over-emphasis, I suppose, is making an emotional mountain out of a colloquial molehill; and under-emphasis is presumably what is called in the theatre "throwing away." Surprise explains itself. I suppose that anything that is irrelevant or divorced from its context, like suddenly shouting or bursting into tears for no reason, would cause comic surprise. A good example of this would be the maid at the end of *George and Margaret* who could only speak in a whisper.

Is this right? Or have I misunderstood your intention? Perhaps it will be easier, now, to take concrete examples of what we are trying to prove, so I am sending you a copy I have made from Granville-Barker's translation of the Anatol play so that you can see how it goes, and perhaps give my friend some practical advice on the playing of the part.

THE WEDDING MORNING

By

'ARTHUR SCHNITZLER

It is a brilliant winter morning. The lately risen sun shines straight into ANATOL's *room.* ANATOL *stands on the hither side of his bedroom door, which is a little open. He is listening. After a moment he closes the door very softly and comes back into the room. He looks nervous and rather puzzled. He sits down on not the most comfortable chair with a fretful sigh. Then he gets up to ring the bell. Then he sits down again. His costume is the strangest mixture of early morning and overnight that ever was: a dressing jacket and dress trousers, slippers, and a scarf round the neck; but he looks bathed and shaved, and his hair is brushed.* FRANZ, *his man, answers the bell and, not seeing him, is going into the bedroom.* ANATOL *jumps up and*

stops him, more by gestures than with his voice,
which he hardly raises above a whisper.

ANATOL: Here, where are you going? I didn't see you.

FRANZ: Did you ring, sir?

ANATOL: Yes . . . bring some breakfast.

FRANZ: Very good, sir.

[*And he is going for it.*

ANATOL: Quietly, you idiot. Don't make such a noise.

[FRANZ *is quiet and apparently comprehending.*
When he is well out of the room ANATOL
makes for the bedroom door again and lis-
tens.

Still asleep!

[FRANZ *comes back with a light breakfast, which*
he puts on the table by the fire saying, very
comprehendingly indeed . . .

FRANZ: Two cups, sir?

ANATOL (*with a look at him*): Yes.

[*A bell rings.* ANATOL *jumps.*

There's someone at the door. At this time in the morning!

[FRANZ *goes out again as quietly.* ANATOL *looks*
round, out of the window, at the bedroom
door, then doubtfully at the teacups, and
says . . .

I don't feel in the least like getting married.

It is a short excerpt, just a page, but I think you will agree that there is plenty of meat for discussion in this alone.

STEPHEN.

21st July 1939.

DEAR JESTING PILATE,

No, I refuse to be drawn into that argument! And now I am going to be firm with you, for I see that this correspondence is developing into a deep intellectual analysis of life, art and fundamentals, and all these things are in my mind far removed from the subject of comedy acting. I admit that I started the line of thought. I expect I just wanted to be clever and dig a little under the surface of the practical craft I have tried to exercise. But now I must insist on one of my dicta if I am to be able to help your young friend; namely that comedy is concerned with the lighter side of life and experience. And if we plunge too far down into the philosophic sea of "truth" and "reality" I shall get out of my depth and drown.

Leaving the definition of truth out of it, but accepting for the pleasure of argument your simile of the Victorian lady, comedy does measure her figure by changing her shape—and changes it by distortion, lack of balance, under- or over-statement and surprise! I mean you to translate your simile into terms of real life and consider why an angular woman is comic in essence—and a fat man amusing to the eye. Imagine Falstaff thin! The author here knew the simple elements of humour in character drawing, and Falstaff's figure is literally over-statement.

Again, take your Victorian lady as truth, and ask her to turn from you and pick up a pin from the floor, so that all you see is her bustle! Here is emphasis laid on one aspect of her without altering her measurements, which is the essence of comedy, vulgar as you may think it! But then laughter is a common thing, an almost physical reaction shared by human beings by virtue of their humanity, not an intellectual concept. And, more-over, I believe that it is excited by different things in different races. National humour can be so different as to be unintelligible to people of another nation. Our own English variety is simple and gentle in essence, the French is a little unpleasant and shocking to us, the American more caustic and sharp, and the Russian so foreign to our mode of thought that I for one shall not discuss it further! Epihodov is probably beyond me, and having given you my point of view about him I shall leave him to you!

I had once a strange experience of the difference in national humour. An Italian play was translated into English.* It was about a man who publicly said that if his wife was unfaithful to him he would kill her, and when, during the action of the play, she is found in circumstances in which she appears to have been unfaith-

* *The Mask and the Face,* English version by C. B. Fernald.

ful, he is forced to act up to his boast and to kill her. However, he cannot bring himself to do this, and instead he sends her away out of the country and pretends to his friends that he has murdered her. He stages a funeral with an empty coffin, and his wife, who is merely amused at his ridiculous behaviour, returns in heavy mourning veils, pretending to be a stranger, and attends her own funeral. He discovers her, and the fun increases as she refuses to go away and he has to hide her in his own house while he receives the admiration of his friends and the officials of the town for his magnificent ruthlessness and strength of character.

We performed this play with great success, treating it as broad comedy, and the husband was played as a figure of fun—a pompous, stupid, conceited fellow. When the Italian author came over to London to see it, I was told that he was horrified at the way it was played, because in his eyes the husband was a serious and interesting character and his predicament should have aroused excitement and sympathy rather than amusement!

Now I come to your statement that in farce "the author merely indicates certain general lines for a character," and therefore you argue that farce is the only kind of comedy acting which should be approached from outside. But farce is only broad comedy. And working backwards I think that my suggestion that the chief element of comedy is lack of proportion is proved by the fact that farce is concerned with the wildest upsetting of balance, the measurements coming nearer to normal in ordinary comedy, nearer still in high comedy, and finally being in proportion in serious drama. And mark you, the acting must observe the same measurements as the author does, broad methods for the broad assumptions of farce, and delicate adjustments for eighteenth-century comedies.

Perhaps I might go so far as to say that almost no gesture or "business" is of itself intrinsically funny, with the exception of a few of the broadest comedy tricks —such as pulling a long nose, winking, or putting on someone else's hat. Generally speaking, comedy or tragedy use the same means to their different ends, for technique is not the thing done but the way of doing it. So that according to the situation the actor uses any truthful exploitation of his material to emphasize the intentions of the author. And in comedy this involves lack of proportion.

Let us get down at last to practical matters and ask your friend to do a few exercises which will show him better than I can explain. First ask him to sit in a chair and imagine a man who may be behind a door intent on murdering him. Tell him to look over his shoulder at the door quickly in fear, then reassure himself that he is safe for the moment. He will find that his whole body and expression is taut—probably his hands clenched to start with. The relaxation will be infinitesimal, for his fear is greater than his temporary reassurance; his expression will be inward, with concentration in his eyes and brow and perhaps a slight frown.

Now ask him instead to imagine a lady in the room behind the door—a light o' love whom he wants to conceal, but who he fears may appear at any moment, having woken up from sleep in his bed. Let him look round quickly in this situation, remembering that her appearance will not be a tragedy to him but merely an inconvenience, a temporary embarrassment, caused by his own folly. His expression will be crumpled, lively with apprehension, showing quick thoughts racing through his mind. His eyes probably restless, his body not taut but twanging like a string that has been plucked. When he looks round it will be a shade more quickly and unsteadily; his whole body will move slightly, his hands will be nervous and looser, and his relief will be quicker too. He may bite his lip a little, as one does in untidy thought, if you know what I mean, for he is undecided how to tackle the situation. This in contrast to the paralysis of fear in the former exercise where one cannot move a muscle.

Please ask Mr. Eager to note that I am not inventing comic business here or being untruthful to the state of mind I wish him to convey. I am simply laying emphasis to one side of the behaviour of an apprehensive man.

Now ask him to suppose himself a nervous little man with a wife of whom he is terrified. His fright is without any foundation; he could stand up to her if he were not disproportionately weak and silly, and she won't really harm him at all. The actor has to lay stress on the lack of proportion between his fear and the reality.

He will now find that his nervousness is shown in little jerky movements. He may bite his nails; as he moves he may knock his elbow on the chair and hurt his funny-bone and forget his fear for a moment in his pain, then remember it again, and listen for his wife with eyes a little too wide open and mouth gaping. When he turns to look over his shoulder he will jump suddenly and may upset his chair and have to save himself from falling. When he is reassured that his wife is not coming at that moment his relief is such that he mops his brow and huddles into his seat and emits a great sigh.

Now all these details are strictly truthful in the situation, but, by being overdrawn and out of relation to the cause, they are in the comic vein, and if done seriously, with truth, will be funny.

Let Mr. Eager try these exercises with you as audience and please report to me the effect he has on you. Remember—he has not got to try to be amusing. He must really believe in the situation and just carry out my instructions in the way he expresses his fright in these three ways.

This brings me to Anatol, for you will find that the second exercise I have suggested will be of use to your friend at once in this part, which is why I chose it. Now in studying this part he must first realize that it is light comedy. When the curtain goes up the audience must immediately get the sense of unrest, of imminent surprise—a taut feeling of uncertainty. The author's directions are that Anatol is nervous and rather puzzled. But

Mr. Eager must on no account confuse this with melancholy or dejection, for this will put the audience in the wrong mood. Inside himself he must be bubbling with the pleasure and excitement of the fun which is coming in the play, not as Anatol, but as Anatol's better self, standing outside him and knowing more about him than Anatol knows of himself. If this sounds too complicated and analytical tell your friend to recall to himself the little excited twist in his diaphragm that he must often have experienced just before he is going to tell someone a funny incident that has happened to him. The telling of the story may have had to be serious in leading up to the point, so he will have kept a straight face, but his inside will have been tingling with the knowledge of the joke to come. Is this clear? The comedy vein has in it the ingredients of high spirits and excitement. (For this reason I like to talk to someone in my dressing room and think gay, irresponsible thoughts before going on for a comedy part. When I am trying to tackle a serious scene I want to be quite quiet before my entrance, to capture the right mood inside. So see that Mr. Eager is tuned up to fun and excitement before he starts his rehearsal of Anatol.)

Now then, his first movements as he listens at the door will be quick and unexpected—a nervous change of posture as he thinks he hears a noise in the bedroom of the girl stirring, his eyes restless, showing sudden twirls of thought as he grapples with the situation in his mind. These things will prepare the audience for the elements of fun, surprise, vitality and slight over-statement to follow.

"He sits down on not the most comfortable chair . . ." Ah, here is a neat exercise in technique! How does one convey this to the audience (who have not tried the chairs or had time to observe their relative comfort) in a flash? Well, one way is this. One sits down with the intention of martyrizing oneself, that is to say one makes oneself as uncomfortable as possible. Let him try the edge of the chair, sitting very upright, shifting slightly to emphasize the chair's hardness, arms tightly to his sides and hands on his knees—feet planted. From this obviously uneasy posture his short audible sigh will have a comic effect or he won't have done it correctly.

Next, his decision to ring the bell must be sudden and slightly surprising—a quick turn of the eyes alone towards the bell as if the idea of ringing it were very important and not an ordinary action. Let him move to it with *empressement* as though he were taking a serious step in ringing it, and sit down again in the same taut way as much as to say, "Now I've tackled this situation."

When Franz comes in, the jump to stop him and the gestures with it must be surprisingly quick and a little overdone—just heightened by a fraction from the normal way of stopping someone from entering a room; and Anatol's desire not to wake the girl by his voice will make his whisper just too sibilant and almost more disturbing than if he spoke in his ordinary voice. He then watches Franz well out of the room, letting his own body go slightly with him (if you understand me) and then goes back to the door on tip-toe more anxiously than before.

"Still asleep!" This with a little shake of the head, a shrug and a look round uneasily for any help possible, though obviously none is there.

" 'Two cups, sir?' 'Yes,' (with a look at him)."

What look? I suggest what is called a withering look —which means a haughty, cold stare—as if he should say, "Don't suggest that it is unusual to have a lady in my room at breakfast." His eyebrows should be slightly raised as in hurt surprise at the question.

Or let him try looking at Franz as man to man with mutual understanding, and saying "Yes" with resignation and dismay as he looks away, slightly shamefaced. Either of these readings will be right and humorous, according as they best suit your friend's personality.

The jump at the bell must be very sharp and end in nervous looks, and perhaps little actions of the hand to the face. The three looks directed by the author, out of the window, at the bedroom door and doubtfully at the teacups, should be punctuated by bringing the head straight again in thought so that full value is given to each action, like a little dance in rhythm. Thus: over the shoulder to the window thinking "Can I escape?" then head round to the front, with puzzled concentra-tion thinking "No, that won't do." Head over the other shoulder towards the door, thinking "Is she still asleep?"

then head back to the front, with apprehensive thought. Finally a sideways glance at the cups, with a slightly shying movement of the body, for the two cups give the position away to a visitor—and the line said as if with nausea and probably a quick closing of the eyes to shut away the situation for a second.

Give this to Mr. Eager as an exercise and see how it comes off. Do not let him imagine it to be the only way to play this scene, but a broad suggestion of the way to attack it from one point of view.

Yours, exhausted!

ATHENE.

19*th November* 1939.

DEAR ATHENE,

So be it. You shall have no more ethical or metaphysical speculations from me. I shall think nothing but "gay, irresponsible thoughts." I shall stop shrouding my arguments in Russian gloom: even Epihodov—since you wish it—shall be allowed to rest in peace. The reason for this? Your horribly persuasive letters, and the fact that I've had time since I last wrote to acquire a little of that "enlarged experience of life and acting" which you say is so conducive to a frivolous mode of thought!

You end your letter "exhausted"—you may well after such a rich spate of ideas!—but I am *beginning* mine exhausted (not, I hasten to say, from reading yours, which was on the contrary most invigorating!). My exhaustion comes from an interview I have been having with friend William. We have been attempting to carry out your suggestions for the first few pages of *Anatol* and the effort has left us both nervous wrecks. I found myself disliking everything he did: and he has disliked me for not being able to tell him why. My difficulty in explaining arose from the fact that he has so little experience of the stage that he does not understand such technical phrases as "ponging," "lifting," "timing" and "throwing away." Possibly I ought not to have used them at all. But I realized to-day, as never before, how much comedy is a matter of practical execution, and how useless it is to theorize about it. I accept the rebuke at the beginning of your last letter, and shall henceforth steer right away from "intellectual analyses of life, art and fundamentals." It is evident to me now that before one can play comedy one must have both a thorough experience of stagecraft and a suitable attitude of mind. Needless to say Mr. Eager has neither, so his performance is apt to be nothing more than a jerky succession of ineffectual good intentions. He cannot, of course, acquire experience of acting overnight but I think he might, with an effort, train himself fairly quickly to approach comedy from the right point of view. I am inclined to think that this comedic sense is not the prerogative of a gifted few but that it can be acquired by any flexible mind; I base my assumption on your theory that knowledge of life can teach it to one, and on my own discoveries which, though not yet far-reaching, have been most encouraging.

One of the greatest practical difficulties, I believe, is to take the audience into one's confidence. One has a natural shyness of them, due perhaps to an excess of good manners in these days when actors are no longer proud of being rogues and vagabonds, but prefer to be *salonfähig* as Schnitzler might have said—that is, "permissible in drawing-rooms."

So many actors nowadays act as if they were aware of being watched and must therefore behave as inconspicuously as possible, for the sake of good manners. It is stupid, of course, but it is so. The tradition of it is almost as strong now—especially with the younger generation—as was the tradition of flamboyance with the actors of fifty years ago. Probably we all of us succumb to it in some degree. William Eager, of course, is swamped by it, since he hasn't the experience to combat it, nor has he known that success which gives a self-assertive edge to one's personality. He acts as if he resented being watched. He gives me the impression that I (as audience) am nothing but an eavesdropper and he even succeeded in making me feel embarrassed at overhearing his conversation! I tried to correct this by making him act as if he were giving an impersonation to "a friend over the port." The effect was rather interesting. His performance became immediately alive and funny. His good intentions were, so to speak, put into practice, and produced a vivid impression. But unfortunately nothing he did or said was as Anatol would have done or said it.

And there, I think, is the rub. It is so difficult to immerse oneself in the character one is playing, as one must even in comedy to a certain extent, and yet retain enough intimacy with an audience to form a basis for the mutual enjoyment of a joke.

Personally I feel that the business of establishing intimacy with an audience is simply a matter of self-confidence; and this might explain why young or in-experienced actors are not effective in comedy. They are not afraid of straight—that is sincere—parts: sincerity has always commanded attention, even from the most hardboiled. But they are pardonably shy of "putting on an act," or setting out to tell a funny story; there is always in the back of their minds the horrible fear that the story may not prove funny after all. This is as true of life as it is of the theatre, and would perhaps account for the case of your "serious beauty" who was unable to acquire a sense of comedy until she reached middle age.

Some of the exercises you suggested were rather beyond William's present grasp of stage technique, and he is still a little vague about the character of Anatol. He may do them better when he knows more of the rest of the play. But one—the "uncomfortable chair" exercise—we dissociated from its context and performed for its own sake. After a little practice he was able to convince me so successfully that my easiest chair was like a fakir's bed of nails that in an absent-minded moment I myself sat on it in intense discomfort. He learned something from this, I think, and laughed at the convincing look of misery on my face, so absurdly out of place when he remembered how comfortable the chair really was.

Of course all these exercises were performed "cold," which made them very difficult for him. It was not possible to tune him up to the fun and excitement he might feel if he were actually going to play the part, and which in fact he did convey in spasms when he played it for his amateur dramatic society. I felt a little cruel at having to tell him he was not being funny, because, of course, it was hard for him to be funny before a necessarily critical and unresponsive person. Next time I think I shall provide him with an audience of enthusiasts like himself, and see whether their anticipation of amusement does not kindle his desire to amuse them. As I say, I think he may succeed far better when he understands the play and can appreciate Anatol's state of mind, when he realizes *why* Anatol "looks round, out of the window, at the bedroom door, then doubtfully at the teacups," and when he has grasped the full significance to Anatol on that particular morning of what is behind the bedroom door.

At present William still thinks of humour as something that exists by itself, some essence which can be snatched out of thin air and put into a performance to make it funny, as one puts cochineal into a blancmange to make it pink. He cannot yet extract humour from lines and situations. Probably it will always be difficult to persuade beginners that actions are not intrinsically funny or tragic. I remember when I was a beginner being told by my teacher to prepare for my next lesson "one tragedy and one comedy gesture." I tried in all seriousness to satisfy her demands and was rather pleased with my idea of beating my forehead for tragedy and scratching my left ear with my right foot for comedy. I regret to say that she found both these "gestures" satisfactory. She must have been a very bad teacher.

In conclusion, what you say about national humour interests me enormously. I find I laugh very rarely at the average English comedy. I am told that this is because I have no sense of humour. I should *so* much prefer to think it was because I happen to be half French! And if ever I find myself sitting unsmilingly through a comedy in France it will be a great consolation to know that this is only because the other half of me is English.

STEPHEN.

9th December 1939.

DEAR STEPHEN,

Your letter gave me immense pleasure, for it seemed to me in reading it that some of the things I had tried to make clear on paper about the craft of comedy acting had really become practical to you and to Mr. Eager.

How right you are about the average Englishman's difficulty in taking the audience into his confidence. As a rule, he has no confidence to take them into! A bad joke, I fear, by which I have startled myself into looking up "confidence" in the *Oxford Dictionary*. It means "firm trust" or "assured expectation" and "the imparting of private matters." So that I see that an actor attempting to be amusing should, firstly, have firm trust in the comedic quality of his part, and secondly, assured expectation that the audience will respond. These will make him able to impart his private opinion (*i.e.* delight in) his interpretation. That should be academic enough even for you! But, in effect, it is the mood of confidence that is so essential in gaining the confidence of the audience, and perhaps that is why I unconsciously try to induce it in myself when I am playing a comedy part, by encouraging gay chatter in my dressing room, releasing myself from outside worries, and generally testing my strength in gaiety before I go on to the stage.

Again, you hit a nail effectively on the head when you say that Mr. Eager missed the encouragement of an audience when he tried the exercises in front of you by yourself.

The audience indeed not only gives one assurance, but positively inspires one's creative impulse. I myself have been studying a new part in a comedy since we began this correspondence, and have had some illuminating experiences. The main point they have re-affirmed for me is that the secret of comic invention is to pay strict attention to one's part and do the things the character would truthfully do in given situations. I will quote you two examples in my own present play. I am a silly little woman very suspicious of the situation in which I find myself—a typical middle-class Englishwoman in a gay French resort. I hear someone asking in French off-stage for a telephone number which I want to remember. The number is *soixante-quinze, quatre-vingt-huit,* and one night I found myself repeating under my breath the first two words with a concentrated expression and then I started quickly to count on my fingers what *quatre-vingt-huit* came to—gave up obviously after about seven and said to myself, "Oh, for heaven's sake, these French numbers!" and then relapsed into injured gloom. It appears to be funny to the audience and I know that the first time I did it it was because when I heard the other character asking for the number I sat up and inclined my head a little towards her, and I felt in my bones that the audience were suddenly interested in my reactions. So that when I heard the number I wanted to show them that I was too stupid to translate it into English and that I shouldn't remember it. This I could never have invented at rehearsal for the situation is not carried further in the plot, and I could (and for the first few nights actually did) merely sit still during the telephone conversation. It needed the audience's warm interest in the scene and in me to bring out this little piece of nonsense. But it was because I felt like a silly little Englishwoman to whom "sixty-fifteen" can never represent "seventy-five" that I managed to get something amusing out of it.

Another lesson my present part is teaching me is the value that one can give to a comic situation by reacting to the other characters in the scene. This is an important part of comedy acting which one can hardly teach to one person alone. Mr. Eager must collect a few friends from his Club to work with—for it is essentially teamwork.

Briefly, no laugh, when two or more characters are on the stage together, can be said to come from one person's efforts—it is nearly always the effect of a line spoken by one and the reactions of the others. I once had this illustrated in my own experience in an exceptional way. I was acting in my youth with an older actor who very obviously disliked his inexperienced young colleague. He could not conceal his disapproval of me, and I was forced at the end of the run to ask him how I had offended him. To my bewilderment he said that my methods of playing a comedy scene were so bad that he had hardly been able to get through the run of the play. I inquired what I had done wrong, and he replied that I always reacted immediately to any line that he spoke to me, explaining that I should have waited for the laugh which his line would get and then react to it and get another laugh. Our scene together was one in which I had to be surprised and shocked at what he said, and, as he pointed out to me, I had been reacting quickly each time he spoke. (I should like to say that, in spite of this, the scene had been punctuated by laughs!)

Our conversation took place on the night before the final performances: we were to finish the play after the evening show on Saturday. I apologized to my elder and better, and at the Saturday matinée I faithfully did as he wanted. I let him say his line each time—then I waited with an impassive face for the expected laugh—and when it did not come I gave my accustomed start of surprise and looked shocked—and again there was no response from the audience! The scene was a complete failure! I avoided my friend after the matinée, and at the evening performance went back, greatly daring, to my other method and heard again the audience's laughter.

I had, in fact, been quite right in my instinct that a laugh arises from the quick reaction of one character to another, and it is often like a rally at tennis—the quicker one returns the impact of a remark, the sooner comes the volley of an audience's pleasure.

This question of the effect of one's reaction was once made very interesting to me when I was playing in a play in which the leading man left and was replaced by another actor. In a certain scene the character they portrayed had to be delightfully shocked at something I said. One of them gave a quick start and then looked at me ₄with pleased amazement immediately I had spoken—and the audience shouted with laughter; the other listened after I had said my line and slowly let a dawning recognition of the meaning of my words creep over his face. The laughter was slow and lacked spontaneity. He had somehow let the ball drop and caught it on the bounce, instead of catching the spectator's breath with a smashing return. Maybe one method is farce and the other comedy, and the first example I have quoted was farce. There was nothing subtle to grow in either the actor's mind or in the scene—it had to be bright and vigorous and a little crude. One of the great difficulties we have to master is to know when comedy is subtle enough to allow of slowing up the pace. This, for instance, applies to Helena's soliloquies in *A Midsummer Night's Dream,* and to Bottom's awakening and, of course, to all Shakespeare's dull-witted clowns.

Then there is the question of "throwing away" a line. This is a delicate operation and can easily end in throwing away the situation! Occasionally a comic retort can be enhanced in effect by a casual delivery, which the audience is just allowed to catch; they think themselves clever because they have had to make a slight effort to understand its point, instead of having it thrown at them. (In passing, let me say that this is a technical accomplishment at which I do not excel!) Another point one has to consider is the bad taste of pursuing a laugh which is irrelevant to the scene in hand. Many comedians succumb to the temptation of being funny in some extraneous way: for a crude example, to blow one's nose loudly, or sneeze, or fall over a mat, when none of these things are directly connected with the part or situation. If the character has a cold in the play then obviously make fun out of the symptoms, but never introduce anything that doesn't illuminate the action of the play or characters.

Comedy mostly demands pace in playing and also the topping of one another's tone. For instance, a character is bullying another, and a third one protests. If the bullying is quick and high in pitch the third character can add to the fun by catching the high, quick voice in his own protest. If the first actor drops the excitement and becomes slowly ponderous he takes away this opportunity. One trick which is legitimate if used with discretion is to change one's mind just before saying a line. This is difficult to explain without an example, but suppose one character accuses another of doing something, the accused can agree absent-mindedly with the accusation in his thought for a fraction of a second and then, realizing its full import, deny it with sudden force. Is this clear and if so will you be so kind as to find an example for Mr. Eager to practise, and let me know results? It's a favourite low comedy trick but, like adversity, can be charming if sweetly used.

Good-bye just now, as they say in Scotland.

ATHENE.

Dear Athene,

We progress.

I have just returned from a performance by William's amateur dramatic club; and yesterday I went to his dress rehearsal. You may imagine what the dress rehearsal was like! Everything was going wrong, but in spite of this there was the usual atmosphere of foolish optimism that it would be "all right on the night." And the play was an undistinguished comedy about a suburban family; I should not have sat it out if I hadn't come specially to see William. His part was effective enough to give him a certain amount of self-confidence and not big enough to swamp him. I discovered a good deal about his difficulties from watching this rehearsal.

What struck me most forcibly was the importance to any actor of a certain degree of pachydermatousness. This may sound an absurd statement when everybody knows that an actor ought to be extremely sensitive. But I believe the two things can be reconciled, otherwise I should find it difficult to explain William's quick understanding in his classes with me and his devil-may-care attitude at yesterday's catastrophic rehearsal. When we work at your exercises our Mr. Eager is receptive and anxious to learn, but shy and not particularly effective in his acting; when he gets into the atmosphere of his club he is opinionated and rather unteachable but extremely telling, in a grand, crude sort of way, upon the stage. I dare say his inferiority complex disappears when he is among his colleagues, who admire his talent. At any rate, he acquires a new confidence, and this has a very powerful effect upon his performance. Clearly, one cannot act well with an inferiority complex, and yet too much self-confidence leads to conceit and unwillingness to listen to criticism. So that I suppose the ideal actor ought to have both an ardour which desires criticism and a nonchalance which refuses to be depressed by it.

William's performance this time was a great improvement upon Anatol. I'm afraid this was partly because he was not flying so high and therefore succeeded more easily in doing what he meant to do; but it also shows that he has benefited from your advice. I was so pleased with his progress that I did not hesitate to take him through his whole part after the rehearsal, going through it almost word by word. It was comparatively simple to explain to him, with the actual example fresh in our minds, what he was doing wrong. He was a little touchy about my spoon-feeding at first, but I wish you had seen him at to-night's performance tentatively putting one or two of my suggestions into practice and finding that they worked.

In one place, where I had shown him how to recover a laugh by a simple inversion of words (he had learned the line incorrectly), he was so surprised when the laugh came that I could actually detect a look of pleasurable amazement growing on his face which was certainly pure William and not in the part at all! Soon after that he abandoned himself entirely to the improvements we had discussed together and I must say that he played the rest of the part pretty well.

Actually, I think what happened to-night was something of a mystery to William. I don't suppose he knows *why* that inversion was more effective; he has never studied the proper balancing of a comedy sentence and he hasn't yet had time to develop a sense of comedic rhythm. He took my advice blindly—ordinarily such a fatal thing to do at a dress rehearsal!—and it turned out to be effective; and the same thing probably applies to the other things, the pauses and moves and stresses which I suggested to him.

I remember an interesting case of an actor losing this "comedic rhythm" during the run of a play, and floundering helplessly about until he found it again. I have forgotten the dialogue which led up to it, but the line which got the laugh was "Nobody asked you." When we had been running a month or two he started to stress this line in an odd way, emphasizing "nobody" instead of "asked" (for some reason). After a few performances he noticed that he had lost the laugh which ought to have followed his remark; and then he began what was (for me) a fascinating chase after that laugh, which lasted for almost three weeks.

He didn't immediately grasp what was wrong with the way he said his line. For several performances he blamed the audience when they didn't laugh. It never occurred to him that, subconsciously, they were disturbed by some oddity in his accentuation of the sentence—(if one analyses it, "*nobody* asked you" has quite a different implication from "nobody *asked* you"). In his effort to "plant" his line he took to saying "Well nobody asked you," as if the extra word gave him a kind of helpful run at his sentence. A week later this had become "Yes, well nobody asked you," and after another week it became "Yes, well nobody *did* ask you!" But none of these variations recaptured the laugh for him.

One night the stage manager noticed that the actor had departed from the original text (if only one had a few more stage managers like this one!), and mentioned it. At the next performance the line was said in the right way—and the laugh returned.

I was pleased to see William not actually winking at the audience but saying his lines well out with more than half a thought of the effect they would have on the house. He overdid it, I fear—the appreciative guffaws went to his head after a time—but as the comedy verged upon the farcical this was not a very grave sin. What was more serious was that his concentration began to stray across the footlights towards us and one huge (and unexpected) laugh overbalanced his control and made him laugh himself. I regret to say that he was quite unable to pull his face straight again and it was lucky that this happened at the very end of an act. I shall send him John Gielgud's book, *Early Stages*, and underline, in red, the passage which goes like this: "It is particularly fatal to succumb in farce (the most tempting kind of play to giggle in) for the absolute seriousness of the actors is usually the very thing which makes the situations funny to the audience."

There was an interesting example in William's play of that "dropping of the tempo" which you referred to in your last letter. The old father and the young cub of a son were having an argument with the daughter about her boy friend. It was three minutes of what one might call quick-fire repartee and ought to have got a laugh every few lines. But it didn't come off because the girl who was playing the daughter, instead of taking the broad tone of the other two, elected to play the part with complete sincerity, and the hesitations, the little movements, the low voice which she used (which would have been charming in a straight scene) simply let the ball drop instead of returning it good and hard to her colleagues.

And again, the woman who played the mother was uncertain of her lines and dithered about with paraphrases, so that the father who, poor man, had to play most of his scenes with her, had great difficulty in scoring his points; he never quite knew when she was going to stop speaking and so couldn't time his replies properly, as you may imagine.

As a writer I am rather interested in this question of phrasing, and I believe it is far more important than

53

most professional actors will allow. Any playwright who knows his stuff (and the author of William's play, with all his faults, does know how to write good comedy dialogue) will balance his sentences most carefully and polish and alter them if necessary at rehearsals so as to give them a good swift rhythm and that "punch" which comedy can't do without. That's why I approve of the stage manager who points out to an actor his deviations from the agreed text; after all, even the most conscientious actor can hardly avoid altering his lines a little during a long run. In my experience this is always a mistake when a play is well written; there are no two ways of saying a good line effectively—there is only the right way or the wrong way. Good comedy dialogue needs the *right word* and the *right rhythm*. Do you agree with me?

Perhaps you can remember a discussion we had when we were both playing in *Candida?* We were talking about those dreadful moments which occasionally come upon one when one forgets a word in the middle of a sentence—especially in dialogue like Shaw's which is not afraid of using rather unaccustomed words. And you said that the great thing to remember in that sort of emergency was to use a word of the same *rhythm* and *number of syllables* as the correct one, if one possibly could think of one in time. In Shakespeare, for instance, one is naturally compelled to do this by the strict rhythm of the verse; but I'm sure you will agree that any good dialogue has its own rhythm, which is as important as the rhythm of a piece of music and should be firmly adhered to.

In conclusion, I got William to practise the exercise you set at the end of your last letter. I believe the films call this sort of trick a "double-take 'em"—is that how one spells it, I wonder? He achieved it—but principally by working his facial muscles and his eyes; in other words, he went at it from the "outside," instead of *thinking* correctly, and letting the two thoughts chase each other across his face. I don't think he has much co-ordination yet between the processes of his mind and the processes of his limbs and muscles. His eyes are an especially feeble feature: he is capable of expressing humour, agony, or love-sickness with his nose, mouth, forehead and ears and yet leaving his eyes quite meaningless. So we have been doing eye exercises. I make him cover up the lower part of his face and "register" the expressions I demand of him with his eyes alone. It is very funny; he usually uses a silk handkerchief, so he looks just as if he is wearing a yashmak.

Incidentally, I noticed when I was in Turkey some years ago that the peasant women all had most expressive eyes but that the lower parts of their faces were heavy and expressionless. As they had only just stopped wearing yashmaks this seems to me rather interesting, and might have meant that disuse of the muscles had robbed them of the power of expression—a warning to lazy actors, don't you agree?

STEPHEN.

Dear Stephen,

I am delighted to hear about young Eager's tussle with the dress rehearsal and all your remarks are so much to the point and your criticism of his work so masterly that I am tempted to turn him over entirely to your guidance now.

Only on one point do I differ from you—when you say that there is only one right way of saying a good line effectively. There are some good lines which can be said two ways with equal point. I've just learnt this from playing in a piece with two different actors, both first rate. Here is the example. In the dialogue the man's daughter discloses the fact that she has been out with his valet the evening before and did not get in till three in the morning. The father accuses her of flirting with the valet; if not, he asks, what were they doing at three o'clock in the morning? She replies indignantly: "He behaved like a perfect gentleman." The father's retort is, "That's what I said."

One actor replied immediately with his line, emphasizing the "I"—"That's what *I* said"—implying that she meant that a perfect gentleman must flirt with a girl to be considered polite and that her remark was intended to convey this: in this case the laugh from the audience was at her discomfiture.

The other actor paused for a moment as if she had convinced him that to be a gentleman meant one *didn't* make advances to a girl—then reconsidered the possible attributes expected of a gentleman in the circumstances and replied very gently: "That's what I *said*." The laugh is just as big, but this time it is at the father's twisting of the girl's meaning. The last way is the subtler, but either way is amusing, and therefore right.

But I agree wholeheartedly that the rhythm of a line is important for comedy effect. The best line is dry and to the point, and any interpolation of "Well" or "Oh" takes away the neatness of a remark.

Your eye exercise sounds great fun. I've never done it. In fact, I have never thought of divorcing one feature of my face from another. This leads me to the question of the use of the whole body in comedy—a side of expression which I often find sadly undeveloped even in professional actors, and quite shockingly neglected by amateurs. How often have pupils of mine tried to play a scene requiring nervous tension while seated cross-legged in a chair in an attitude of relaxation—an obvious impossibility; and, of course, only attempted because they were not acting at all, but merely saying lines. (That would make an interesting exercise: to try to say angry words with a slack body, or a line of dignified protest while lolling on a sofa! The words could not help sounding insincere. That is one of my reasons for hating the practice of reading parts at a first rehearsal sitting round a table, because of the intense difficulty of not suiting the action to the word!)

I am now playing a part which might be described as an essay in indignation. I am outraged from my first entrance to my final exit. In order not to become too monotonous I have had recourse to using my feet, my hands and my shoulders to help me vary similar situations. I lock my hands back to back and twist them palm to palm as I pace round the stage; I hold my back very straight like a ramrod; I outline the pattern on my dress with an irritated forefinger; I bang my feet together sharply at one point when I am sitting down. All these things should have an intrinsically comic effect that helps the part. In *Candida* I used the typewriter as though I were playing a cadenza (as someone said) in Prossie's scene of irritation with Burgess. But these things must only be done when the audience's interest is centred on one's own part, otherwise one is in danger of distracting their attention from what they are supposed to be looking at.

I ought perhaps to make it clear that none of the aforesaid pieces of "business" were in any sense thought-out, and probably not all of them were used in rehearsal. They sprang out of my endeavours to express myself in the character when acting, and then I noted them as an observer and retained them consciously. In playing comedy I am sure one has to rely first on the subconscious or inspirational method of reading a part by sinking oneself in the character, and then check the results consciously from outside oneself and keep what seems good, and discard what is overdone or what misses fire. It's a kind of dual control of one's performance.

Now, should we continue with our analysis of Anatol

for Mr. Eager's benefit? He will probably be feeling his comedian's feet a little more since the first exercise if he has followed our discussion on pace and the use of legitimate "business," and also the amplifying of a part by the characteristic use of the body. You will have to ask a friend now to play Max. This—with slight cuts— is how the dialogue goes.

> [*In bursts* MAX, *in the best of spirits;* FRANZ *behind, looking as if he ought to have stopped him.*

MAX: My dear fellow!

ANATOL: Tsch! . . . don't talk so loud. Get another cup, Franz.

MAX *(at the table):* Two cups here already.

ANATOL: Get another cup, Franz, and then get out.
> [FRANZ *obeys with discretion.* ANATOL *is very fretful.*

ANATOL: What are you doing here at eight o'clock in the morning?

MAX: Nearly ten!

ANATOL: Well . . . what are you doing here at ten o'clock in the morning?

MAX: It's my wretched memory.

ANATOL: Don't talk so loud!

MAX: I say . . . you're very jumpy. What's the matter?

ANATOL: Yes . . . I am very jumpy.

MAX: But not to-day.

ANATOL: Oh . . . what is it you want?

MAX: You know your cousin Alma's to be my bridesmaid at the wedding. About her bouquet . . .

ANATOL (with rather sulky indifference): What about it?

MAX: I forgot to order it, and I forgot to ask her what colour she's wearing. What do you think . . . white or red or blue or green?

ANATOL: Certainly not green!

MAX: Are you sure?

ANATOL: You know she never wears green.

MAX: How do I know?

ANATOL: Don't shout! It's nothing to be excited about.

MAX (a little exasperated): Do you know what colour she will be wearing at your wedding this morning?

ANATOL: Yes . . . red or blue.

MAX: Which?

ANATOL: What does it matter?

MAX: Damn it . . . for the bouquet.

ANATOL: You order two . . . you can wear the other in your hair.

MAX: That's a silly joke.

ANATOL (his head on his hand): I'll be making a sillier in an hour or two.

MAX: You're a cheerful bridegroom . . . I must say!

ANATOL: Well . . . I've been very much upset.

MAX: Anatol . . . you're hiding something.

ANATOL (with great candour): Not at all.

[*From the bedroom rings a female voice, loud and clear.*

THE VOICE: Anatol!

[*In the silence that follows* MAX *looks at* ANATOL *in something more than surprise.*

ANATOL (*casually*): Excuse me a minute.

[*He goes and gingerly opens the bedroom door. A pretty pair of arms appears and rests upon his shoulders. In answer to the embrace, for a moment his head disappears. He shuts the door then and returns to his scandalized friend.*

Max should enter with a beaming smile and a light step. Let him go quickly over to Anatol and give him a sound slap on the back. (I am suggesting broad methods for these exercises, for it is well that beginners should overdo everything to start with. One can always pull down a performance, but it is difficult to increase the stature of acting once it has begun on small lines.) Now ask Mr. Eager to react to the slap on the back and then say "Sh-h" with aggravation added to fear of being overheard. "Don't talk so loud" should be an exaggerated whisper. "Get another cup, Franz," testily—said primarily to get Franz out of the way. All through this, see that Franz is registering repressed amusement and excitement at the situation—his attention riveted on Anatol to see what he will do. Anatol's next line "Get another cup, Franz," in a higher tone, with a stony look and a great distinctness on the words "and *then— get out.*" Franz adopts at once the perfect valet's demeanour, taking all expression out of his face, and exits.

Now the next scene between Anatol and Max must be picked up as the door closes behind Franz (both men watching his exit) with pace, quickly catching up cues all the way through right away to the girl's voice calling "Anatol." I should let Anatol walk nervously about the room, passing the bedroom door as he says, "Don't talk so loud," with a stiffening of his body as if preparing for danger. The "Oh" is exasperated and quick. "Don't shout," with a nervous gesture of protest: his whole demeanour nervous and irritable. Max remains static, easy, with a slightly puzzled expression, but never takes his eyes off Anatol. But he must keep up the pace all through.

The voice calling "Anatol" must produce in contrast a slow reaction from both the men. Anatol stops walking about and is frozen into rigidity, and slowly turns his face from Max's gaze. Max half turns his head to the door from which the voice came and then slowly back to Anatol's averted face with a look of growing understanding, tinged with suppressed amusement. This slowing down after the quick fire of the preceding dialogue should be effective.

Then Anatol elaborately relaxes his tension and with slightly forced casualness goes to the door on his line— "Excuse me a minute," spoken most naturally and easily. After the embrace (which must be watched by Max with increasing astonishment, bending forward to see better) Anatol must close the door neatly and with care, not hurriedly, then lean back against it with a touch of bravado.

MAX: Well, really, Anatol!

ANATOL: Let me explain.

MAX: If this is how you begin your married life!

ANATOL: Don't be an ass.

MAX: I'm not a moral man myself, but, hang it all!

ANATOL: Will you let me explain?

MAX (*looking at his watch*): Hurry up, then ... your wedding's at half-past twelve.

ANATOL: So it is!

[*He sits silent for a moment; then slowly begins ...*

Last night I was at my father-in-law's ... my future father-in-law's.

MAX: I know that. I was there.

ANATOL: So you were ... I forgot. You were all there. You were all very lively. There was lots of champagne. A lot of you drank my health ... and Sophia's health.

MAX: I drank your health ... and her health ... and wished you both happiness.

ANATOL: So you did. Happiness! Thank you very much.

MAX: You thanked me last night.

ANATOL: They kept it up till past twelve.

63

MAX: I know. I kept it up.

ANATOL: They kept it up till really . . . I thought I was happy.

MAX: Well . . . that's enough about that.

ANATOL: . . . We broke up about half-past twelve, didn't we? I gave Sophia a kiss . . . and she gave me a kiss. No . . . she gave me an icicle. My teeth just chattered with it as I went downstairs.

MAX: So what did you do?

ANATOL: So I thought I'd go to the ball at the Opera.

MAX: Oho!

ANATOL: And why not? . . . They were in full swing at the Opera. I watched for a bit. Oh . . . that swish of a silk petticoat! And don't a girl's eyes shine through a mask? It makes her neck look so white. Then I just plunged into it all. I wanted to breathe in the sound and the scent of it . . . to bathe in them.

MAX (consulting his watch again): Time's getting on. What happened then?

ANATOL: Was I drunk with champagne at papa-in-law's?

MAX: Not a bit.

ANATOL: I got drunk with that dancing . . . mad drunk. It was my Opera ball . . . given on purpose to say good-bye to poor bachelor me! I say! . . . you remember Katinka?

MAX: Green-eyed Katinka?

ANATOL: Sh-h!

64

[MAX *points to where the voice came from.*

MAX: Is that Katinka?

ANATOL: No, it just isn't Katinka. Green-eyes was there, though! And a pretty dark girl called . . . no, never you mind about her. . . . I could tell them all through their masks. I knew their voices. . . . I knew their ankles. One girl I wasn't sure about. And whether I was running after her or she after me . . .? But something in the way she swung her shoulders . . .! And we met and we dodged, and at last she caught me by the arm . . . and then I knew her right enough.

Now that the cat is out of the bag Anatol is relaxed from tension and the preceding scene can be played with ease and slower, and with a sense almost of pride in the telling of the story. It needs a kind of bitter exaggeration with easy, slow gestures to point it, the tempo and the mood quite changed from his previous one of taut nervousness. Max must provide the tension: his mood has changed from ease to stiffness. Anatol will be better seated. Max should stand rather rigidly; his interjections must be thrown in dryly on the surface of the almost indifferent casual recital of Anatol—a legato theme with pizzicato accompaniment.

Anatol warms up to the tale of his adventures when he mentions Katinka, and his pace and lightness must increase in the long speech about the ball. He must half smile, right up to the line "and at last she caught me by the arm," which is said with excitement: then a pause, and in a slower, flat voice "and then I knew her right enough"—as if to suggest "Fate!" He can shake his head and relapse into a despondent attitude.

[MAX *points again.*
MAX: Lona?
ANATOL: Tsch!
MAX: What . . . not even Lona?
ANATOL: Lona right enough . . . don't fetch her in yet. We went and sat under a palm. Back again . . . she said. Yes . . . I said. When? . . . she said. Not till last night. Why haven't you written . . . where on earth have you been? Off the map . . . I said . . . but I'm back again, and I love you still. And don't I love you still? . . . she said. And the waiter brought the champagne. We were very happy.
MAX: Well . . . I'm blessed.
ANATOL: Then we got into a cab . . . Just as we used to. She put her head on my shoulder. Never to part, she said . . . and went to sleep. We didn't get back till seven. She's still asleep . . . was, when you came.
[*The story over, he sits contemplating the world generally with puzzled distress.* MAX *jumps up.*
MAX: Anatol . . . come to your senses.
ANATOL: Never to part! And I've got to be married at half-past twelve!
MAX: Yes . . . to somebody else.

66

ANATOL: Isn't that just like life? It's always some-body else one gets married to.

MAX: You ought to change . . . you've not much time.

ANATOL: I suppose I'd better. (*He studies the bed-room door doubtfully, and then turns to his friend.*) You know . . . looked at in a certain light this is pathetic.

MAX: It's perfectly disgraceful.

ANATOL: Yes . . . it is disgraceful. But it's very pathetic, too.

MAX: Never mind that . . . you hurry up.

Now the full horror of the plight he is in has come over him and the speech beginning "Lona right enough" must be said quickly again in a dull, almost monotonous voice with little, loose movements of the hands to show his helplessness in the situation. A slight pause after "the waiter brought the champagne"—perhaps a sigh —and then, "We were very happy," delivered with great lugubriousness, so that the despairing expression contrasts comically with the words.

Max should now relax his taut position and stretch himself, saying slowly, "Well, I'm blessed." Anatol delivers his next speech in the same lifeless way. There is a pause. Suddenly Max breaks the scene with a quick, sharp voice, even shaking Anatol by the shoulder, as if he were waking a sleep-walker. Now Anatol must begin to lose his numbness and his position will shift—he has probably slumped forward in his chair with hands hanging limply between his knees. He gradually recovers the pace on "never to part" and "I've got to be married at half-past twelve," rumpling his hair with his hand and rising to his feet. Max holds him firmly by the arm. "Yes—to somebody else," speaking clearly and admonishingly. Anatol speaks like a child up into Max's face, "Isn't that like life?" Then a little wildly on a higher tone, "It's always somebody else one gets married to." Max drops his arm and says firmly, "You ought to change," like Fate speaking. Anatol drops the pace again on "I suppose I'd better." I should let him take a step towards the bedroom door, and then turn back to say, "You know, looked at in a certain light this is pathetic"—very sorry for himself and enjoying being a martyr. Max, stiffly and with emphasis, "It's perfectly disgraceful" (contrast between a limp demeanour on Anatol's part and righteous stiffness from Max's body). Anatol replies impersonally: "Yes, it is disgraceful—but it's very pathetic too"—a little overdone in his sorrow for himself to show that the situation is not really serious.

Max must pick up the scene now for Lona's entrance, with quick irritation—"Never mind that—you hurry up," with a gesture of impatience. The whole exercise here is change of tempo and mood, and contrast of character; for the scene is really holding up the action of the play, and if it is not broken up it will become boring to the audience, who are all the time waiting for the *dénouement*.

I think perhaps we have done enough of *Anatol* now,

and for exercise in a three-cornered scene and in team-work I shall choose something totally different next time. I want Mr. Eager to get used to other methods of attack.

Yours ever,

ATHENE.

10*th February* 1940.

DEAR ATHENE,

Well: we have done your exercises from *Anatol,* and I think that William's theoretical education begins to near completion. What he obviously needs most now is practical acting, and lots of it. His chief fault still is a kind of "smudginess," an uncertainty as to what he means to do and how he means to do it, which very often kills the effect of his acting. Only practice I am sure can give him this sharp edge which his work still needs; practice and self-confidence, and perhaps a little success to be going on with. I have been trying to persuade him, since he genuinely wants to go on the stage, to throw up his job at the bank and try to get work in a Repertory Company. Fortunately he has a couple of hundred pounds saved to keep him going until something comes along. I don't feel as wicked, after having given him this advice, as I expected to. There are many far less talented people than he on the stage. But what I believe is of greatest importance is his *mentality.* It is very much the actor's. He is adaptable, eager to learn, hard-working and suffers enviably little from those inhibitions with which so many of us are burdened. Also, he is fast acquiring (or perhaps simply developing) a pleasantly frivolous attitude towards life which ought, you say, to help his comedy, and which may certainly help him over the more sordid incidents of life in provincial "digs." He is not, I think, interested in "comedy" in the abstract: he says he wants to act and enjoys making people laugh. How he does it isn't of much importance to him. (I hope it will be one day!) Still, he asked me one very pertinent question when we were discussing repertory theatres. He said he might be called on to do a "period" play, a Restoration Comedy, say, or a Sheridan: if so, how was he to tackle it? Was he to remember all you had told him, or forget it, as one hastily discards one's stage technique when one goes on to a film floor?

As I'm no authority on period comedy, I answered rather cautiously so as not to queer your pitch; but actually it seems to me that the principles of playing comedy remain fundamentally the same, whatever the play. In saying this, I am aware that I am withdrawing from the position I held at the beginning of this correspondence, when I thought that each form of acting should be rigorously differentiated.

We have agreed that the principles of comedy are distortion, contrast, surprise; and as it seems to me that one might meet these things in any play from Aristophanes to Lonsdale, I suggested to William Eager that he should try and make use of them whatever comedy he happens to be playing in, provided of course he didn't violate the style or period of the play. Was I wrong?

One other thing I noticed: the scene you quoted from *Anatol* was chiefly for two characters, so that William and the friend who rehearsed it with him were able to "take it in turns" to be funny, so to speak. But they don't yet realize that one cannot be funny by oneself; and they missed a good deal of the humour by each acting in a water-tight compartment of his own. This meant that they never led up properly to each other's laughs and also that one of them occasionally "trod on" the other's laughs by not being aware of the part he himself was playing in that laugh. For instance, in the scene of the embrace, William was so anxious to appear comic that he thoroughly overdid the embracing; this was disturbing to watch because, of course, the audience's interest should have been principally centred on Max. Comedy could only come if Anatol were behaving so casually as (*a*) not to distract our attention from Max, and (*b*) to give an added point to Max's astonishment. Anatol thus also robbed himself of the comedy of his subsequent affectation of nonchalance.

The line about the champagne went very well, William's dejected face and delivery contrasting well with the gaiety of its meaning. This reminds me of one of my own earliest discoveries about comedy, namely, that it often arises out of what I call "anti-modal" actions or remarks: that is to say, that although an actor is deeply

71

sunk in one particular mood, he suddenly says or does something which calls up a totally different one. The effectiveness of this particular kind of comedy, I think, lies in the fact that it often calls up a gulp as well as a laugh; as, for example, in that film of Deanna Durbin's, where she asks her young engineer boy friend, just after he first kisses her, "What *is* a Diesel?" Or the more cruel example of the man who knew his mistress was tired of him because, as he began to make love to her, she absent-mindedly picked up a book. It is perhaps the kind of comedy that you extracted from that performance of *The Mask and the Face*—where the woman goes to her own funeral—which, you say, so horrified the author!

When you say that it is impossible to speak angry words with a slack body are you not thinking of straight acting rather than comedy? Did we not agree that contrast—what I call "anti-modality"—was one of the basic principles of comedy? Is this not the very kind of situation which makes a play like *The Importance of Being Earnest* so funny—the fact that John Worthing and Algernon Moncrieff can fight tooth and nail while devouring muffins?

JACK: How you can sit there, calmly eating muffins when we are in this horrible trouble, I can't make out. You seem to me to be perfectly heartless.

ALGERNON: Well, I can't eat muffins in an agitated manner. The butter would probably get on my cuffs.

One should always eat muffins quite calmly. It is the only way to eat them.

JACK: I say it's perfectly heartless your eating muffins at all, under the circumstances.

ALGERNON: When I am in trouble, eating is the only thing that consoles me. . . . At the present moment I am eating muffins because I am unhappy. Besides, I am particularly fond of muffins.

And the "mislaying" of a baby—a matter of vital importance anyhow to the baby—can be put right by Lady Bracknell seated commandingly on a drawing-room sofa with no more "flap" than if she were rearranging a miscalculated dinner menu. We get our fun out of just these inconsequences, out of the fact that everything is just *not* as it would have been in real life. The result may, as you suggest, be insincere: but that is where the comedy lies.

Yours ever,

STEPHEN.

29*th March* 1940.

DEAR STEPHEN,

Your letter brings up a very interesting point, for I believe we shall find that your reference to period plays and to "anti-modal" acting, as well as your quotation from *The Importance of Being Earnest,* all have bearing on the same thing—namely artificial or high comedy as distinct from straight comedy. As I see it, straight comedy is closely allied in spirit and execution to straight serious acting, but artificial comedy is a thing apart. If I try to put into words certain broad distinctions and fundamental characteristics I am afraid they may appear portentous, but I must not be afraid of this, and if you can extract any truth from them and transmit it to Mr. Eager I shall be glad.

In general terms then, I would say that there are three categories of dramatic expression. Firstly poetry, secondly straight drama and comedy, and thirdly artificial or high comedy. They all deal with human experience. But poetic drama measures human experience by eternal truths, by spiritual values; drama and comedy measure human experience by standards of human nature; and high comedy measures it by manners and customs. In poetic drama one's interpretation must always be governed by the underlying philosophy of the play. Poetry demands something more than faithful delineation of character and situation. Straight drama or comedy demands simply truthful interpretation of human characteristics, heightened by exaggeration and "point of view" as we have discussed in these letters, but having its roots in universal human qualities. But in artificial comedy the chief concern of playwright and actor is the external manners of a given period which, though superficial, yet deeply affect behaviour; and from these the comedy springs.

So you have Restoration comedies, eighteenth-century plays, nineteenth-century comedies of manners, and more recently Noel Coward's and Lonsdale's light modern plays, all of which deal with the "surprise, contrast and disproportion" of people's actions seen against the conventions of their various periods. These plays are necessarily a little more superficial in type, but none the less amusing and illuminating, and for that very reason they call for a different style of execution from that used in straight comedy acting. They need the lightest touch and the most detached point of view, for they deal with externals. *The Importance of Being Earnest* is one of the greatest examples of this type of comedy and concerns itself with the conventions of society of its time. It shows the absurdities of the well-bred, cynical, easy manner of the "upper classes" with its levelling of all emotion and experience to apparent indifference, its correct attitude for the *ingénue*, the glossing over of what lies beneath "Bunburying," and, in the very passage you quote, it is this polite custom of not taking anything seriously which makes the eating of muffins as important as the discussion of troubles.

Again, in the seventeenth century, the manners of the times, liberated from the violent Puritanism of the Commonwealth, expressed contempt of discipline in sex matters; and an illicit love-affair or the cuckolding of an old husband or the licentious exploits of the hero actually were not considered shocking, or indeed of more importance than a good dinner or any other pursuit of pleasure. The comedy lies in the lack of proportion between the things done and the way in which the custom of the times regarded them.

In the eighteenth-century play *The School for Scandal* the manners of the times are consciously held up to ridicule in certain scenes, and one gets the artificial comedy on one side centering round Joseph and Lady Sneerwell, contrasted with true natural comedy in the Teazle scenes.

Therefore, from the angle of the actor portraying a character in one of these artificial comedies, the first essential is to try to realize the manners of the period. For instance, briefly: the gay licentiousness of *The Country Wife* is expressed in the women by the low-cut dresses to display their "charms," the use of the fan for provocative glances above it, the deep curtsey to display to the full their bare shoulders and frivolously shaking curls, and a breadth of gesture, of turn and of inviting poses. In the case of the men: a lace handkerchief flirted as they bow with an exaggerated interest in their women, the consciousness of a well-turned leg displayed to full advantage, and an almost studied sense of ease and flamboyancy in gesture which springs from the consciousness that there is no limit set to their gallantry. The very clothes and the wigs of this period encourage the appropriate bearing, and woe to the actor who looks for trouser pockets in which to bury his expressionless hands, or a cigarette with which to keep them busy! It would be a good exercise for Mr. Eager to rehearse a Wycherley comedy in costume to accustom himself to the demands it will make on him. In the modish characters of the eighteenth century there was even a conscious affectation, shown for example in the use of a spy-glass held up to a perfectly sound eye, and in the elaborate gestures of taking out a snuff-box, tapping it, and flicking possible dust from embroidered waistcoats. To lean gracefully back in an armchair with one well-stockinged leg posed over the other carries out the fashionable manner of the eighteenth century, whereas a similar position in a modern comedy may well merely denote a cad. So much difference does the point of view of a period involve.

The nineteenth century, as a contrast, begins to develop modesty in the women and a certain stiffness and correctness of attitude in the men. A lady of 1840 would never cross her legs (indeed this was a cardinal rule when I first went on the stage in 1909!) whereas the twentieth-century young woman adopts this attitude quite normally in a tailored suit or slacks. The men of the Victorian era naturally sat very upright and uneasily because of the exigencies of their tight trousers; besides, good manners forbade lounging in any way.

Deportment was cultivated in both sexes. I wish it could be cultivated a little more nowadays. The modern girl who has round shoulders and stands with all her weight thrown down on a depressed stomach looks horrible in the skirt and shirt-blouse of 1890. The skirt sags from the blouse behind, and all the trim primness of high collar and neat waist are lost. Let a modern actress wear whalebone corsets underneath these clothes and she will soon learn how to carry them.

The very steps taken in walking vary in different periods; and I should say that woman ought to *dance* as she moves in a seventeenth-century play, to *sail* in an eighteenth-century one, to *swim* in a nineteenth-century dress (with tiny, even steps under crinoline or bustle) and to *stride* in the twentieth century. Roughly, then, she wouldn't be out of period.

Shall we analyse a little scene from some Restoration comedy for Mr. Eager and perhaps a girl friend? Let me know and I will choose one.

Yours ever,

ATHENE.

18th April 1940.

DEAR ATHENE,

I'm fascinated by your letter. It's an essay in itself, and seems to me to say the last word on how to play English "period" comedy. It's a relief to find (as in fact I've always suspected) that the thing is so comparatively simple. So much nonsense is taught to our students in the schools about the difficult mysteries of period comedy; and no doubt most of us carry this mumbo-jumbo about with us for a long time before we get a chance to try our hands at the real thing. I hope your letter will let a little fresh air into the minds of those who are still befuddled with the wrong ideas. William Eager will certainly profit by it. We discussed it yesterday, and, for a practical lesson, spent the afternoon at Nathan's trying on the clothes of each period. I ought to mention that the "class" now contains four pupils— two men besides William and one girl. They have arranged to hire costumes of the Restoration for a Sunday evening which we are to spend in practising period deportment.

I think perhaps, when the time comes, I shall get them to read a scene from a play—say *Love for Love*. They will find it easier if they have lines to say and a definite plot to carry out. There is a rather good scene— do you remember it?—Scene II in the first act, where Mrs. Frail comes to visit Valentine. I wonder if you'd have time to write down a few notes on how we ought to tackle this scene? I shall feel happier with you to guide me; if I rely on my own feelings about Congreve I shall probably imbue my luckless young friends with apocryphal ideas, and so unwittingly contribute to the already large stores of mumbo-jumbo in their brains. I'll copy out the scene in case you haven't got it by you. I have cut parts of it as it is rather too long for our purposes.

Incidentally, I might add that we have not been idle since we received your last letter, and that all four of my pupils are beginning to acquire what I should like to call "theatrical intelligence." They very quickly grasp what I want them to do and, better still, are learning to convey it. So you need not be afraid, in your notes, of asking too much of them. They've reached a stage at which the more one asks of them the more they give.

Yours ever,

STEPHEN.

20th *April* 1940.

DEAR STEPHEN,

It is not easy to give directions on paper for the playing of seventeenth-century plays, for the interest lies mainly in verbal wit, and there is little emphasis laid on naturalistic details pointing to the practical life of the characters. The stage directions go no further mostly than to state the place of the action and occasionally add that the characters are seated or reading. Therefore one cannot help the actors much by inventing "business," as is possible in modern plays, for the fashionable folk of the Restoration period as shown in their plays seemed to do nothing but exercise their wit! Everything, then, must depend on manner of delivery and of pose and of quick passing of thought in the mind of the actor.

Take, for instance, the scene you have chosen in Congreve's *Love for Love*. It is very broad in writing, but typical of the manners of the period, which combined in high society licentiousness of behaviour with an affectation of manners and complete frivolity in matters of morals. So that the actors must deliver the unpleasant lines and innuendoes without any hint of finding them improper according to the standards of 1940. Coarse expressions and frankness were accepted as part of the fashionable convention of the day, and if they are said with complete confidence they will be only amusing and not shocking to a present-day audience. If, however, the actor tries to slur them over or shies at them he will embarrass the spectators because he will obtrude his own modern, moral censure on the looser convention of the seventeenth century.

Congreve sums up the characters for one's guidance in the "Dramatis Personæ." They are as follows:

VALENTINE (*fallen under his father's displeasure by his expensive way of living, in love with Angelica*).

SCANDAL (*his friend, a free speaker*).

TATTLE (*a half-witted beau, vain of his amours, yet valuing himself for secrecy*).

MRS. FRAIL (*a woman of the town*).

One has only to add that Valentine is the charming, gay young man-about-town—the Anatol of those times—and that Scandal is a philosopher in his way and a person of mordant wit and an observer of current manners and weaknesses. He is a deeper character than the others and a kind of "melancholy Jacques" of the period. Now for your scene from the play, which I will analyse bit by bit.

ACT I—SCENE II

TATTLE: Valentine, I supped last night with your mistress and her uncle—old Foresight. I think your father lies at Foresight's.

VALENTINE: Yes.

TATTLE: Upon my soul, Angelica's a fine woman—and so is Mrs. Foresight, and her sister, Mrs. Frail.

SCANDAL: Yes, Mrs. Frail is a very fine woman; we all know her.

TATTLE: Oh, that is not fair!

SCANDAL: What?

TATTLE: To tell.

SCANDAL: To tell what? Why, what do you know of Mrs. Frail?

TATTLE: Who, I? Upon honour, I don't know whether she be man or woman—but by the smoothness of her chin, and roundness of her hips.

SCANDAL: No?

TATTLE: No.

SCANDAL: She says otherwise.

TATTLE: Impossible!

SCANDAL: Yes, faith. Ask Valentine else.

TATTLE: Why, then, as I hope to be saved, I believe a woman only obliges a man to secrecy that she may have the pleasure of telling herself.

SCANDAL: No doubt on't. Well, but has she done you wrong, or no? You have had her? Ha?

TATTLE: Though I have more honour than to tell first, I have more manners than to contradict what a lady has declared.

SCANDAL: Well, you own it?

TATTLE: I am strangely surprised! Yes, yes, I can't deny't, if she taxes me with it.

SCANDAL: She'll be here by-and-by—she sees Valentine every morning.

TATTLE: How?

VALENTINE: She does me the favour, I mean, of a visit sometimes. I did not think she had granted more to anybody.

SCANDAL: Nor I, faith; but Tattle does not use to belie a lady; it is contrary to his character. How one may be deceived in a woman, Valentine!

TATTLE: Nay, what do you mean, gentlemen?

SCANDAL: I'm resolved I'll ask her.

TATTLE: O barbarous! Why! Did you not tell me—

SCANDAL: No, you told us.

TATTLE: And bid me ask Valentine?

VALENTINE: What did I say? I hope you won't bring me to confess an answer, when you never asked me the question?

TATTLE: But, gentlemen, this is the most inhuman proceeding——

VALENTINE: Nay, if you have known Scandal thus

83

long, and cannot avoid such a palpable decoy as this was, the ladies have a fine time whose reputations are in your keeping.   [*Re-enter* JEREMY

JEREMY: Sir, Mrs. Frail has sent to know if you are stirring.

VALENTINE: Show her up when she comes.

[*Exit* JEREMY

TATTLE: I'll be gone.

VALENTINE: You'll meet her.

TATTLE: Is there not a back way?

VALENTINE: If there were, you have more discretion than to give Scandal such an advantage; why, your running away will prove all that he can tell her.

TATTLE: Scandal, you will not be so ungenerous? Oh, I shall lose my reputation of secrecy for ever!—I shall never be received but upon public days; and my visits will never be admitted beyond a drawing-room: I shall never see a bed-chamber again, never be locked in a closet, nor run behind a screen, or under a table; never be distinguished among the waiting-women by the name of trusty Mr. Tattle more.—You will not be so cruel.

VALENTINE: Scandal, have pity on him; he'll yield to any conditions.

TATTLE: Any, any terms.

SCANDAL: Come, then, sacrifice half a dozen women of good reputation to me presently.—Come, where are you familiar?—and see that they are women of quality, too, the first quality.

TATTLE: 'Tis very hard. Well, first then——

84

TATTLE: O unfortunate! she's come already; will you have patience till another time;—I'll double the number?

SCANDAL: Well, on that condition. Take heed you don't fail me.

At the beginning of this scene the men are disposed about the stage in the easy attitudes of men talking intimately together. Scandal is perhaps stretched on a settee, feet up on the arm. Valentine may be in a chair with legs thrust out in front of him and feet crossed. Tattle, who is extravagantly dressed, corseted and obviously made-up, is leaning negligently on the overmantel of the fireplace. Tattle's delivery must be full of affectation, mincing and effeminate and high-pitched. Valentine has an open, amiable manner, and Scandal should suggest sarcasm and misanthropy, wearing darker clothes and having a quieter manner. He should often have a little twisted smile, and a fastidious way of selecting his words without emphasis when he speaks.

Tattle, in a fatuous way, remarks on his women friends, probably at the same time arranging the frills at his wrist, when Scandal breaks in more slowly and with meaning: "Yes, Mrs. Frail is a very fine woman; we all know her." (Mrs. Frail, as Congreve tells us, is a woman of the town.)

Tattle utters a little scream of affected, insincere protest—"Oh, that is not fair!"

Scandal, lazily, with a smile of triumph at succeeding in baiting Tattle, asks "What?"

Tattle, with false righteousness: "To tell"—perhaps using a little silly gesture with his forefinger raised as if in admonition.

Scandal, pursuing his game with confident malice: "To tell what?" then rousing himself and sitting up: "Why, what do you know of Mrs. Frail?" He is pulling a bow at a venture, so there must be a double edge to this question, suspicion and accusation—will Tattle give himself away?

Tattle's next lines in a flurry and with quickened pace, obviously lying.

Scandal gets up from the settee with a little laugh: "No?"

Tattle, moving from the mantelpiece to a chair and sitting petulantly: "No."

Scandal, backing from Tattle and fixing him with an amused stare: "She says otherwise"—words spaced out with gentle emphasis.

Tattle leaps up from his chair really surprised by this. "Impossible."

Scandal, airily, with a meaning look at Valentine: "Yes, Faith. Ask Valentine else." Valentine gives Scandal a look of repressed amusement and admonition which must suggest to the audience that all this is invention on Scandal's part—a shot in the dark to take Tattle unawares.

Tattle, completely taken in, says his next line with

real annoyance at having, as he thinks, kept a secret which has been given away by the partner to it. It is a petulant annoyance, accompanied by a little weak gesture, perhaps a stamp of the foot.

Scandal, frankly amused, presses his next question with malice to be sure that he has hit the mark.

Tattle assumes an air of false chivalry and tries to recover himself on the next line—a little anxiously, as if thinking, "Did she really give me away?" And when Scandal presses him he finally gives in with smug complacency in his conquest.

Scandal, having extorted his information, moves away with a look of triumph exchanged with Valentine as he throws off the remark, "She will be here by-and-by—she sees Valentine every morning."

Tattle is now really rattled. Valentine's disclaimer has overdone innocence in it—he and Scandal assuming astonishment at what they suspected to be true all the time. "How one may be deceived in a woman, Valentine!" with mock indignation.

Tattle tumbles to the trap he has fallen into: "Nay, what do you mean, gentlemen?" is said pettishly, and if they are one on each side of him he should turn his head from one to the other with little ineffectual movements and pursed lips.

Scandal, hardly controlling his laughter: "I'm resolved I'll ask her."

Tattle, with a shrill scream: "Oh barbarous! Why! Did you not tell me——?"

Scandal, dryly: "No, you told us."

Tattle, quickly: "And bid me ask Valentine?"

Valentine, frankly laughing: "And what did I say?" (accent on "did").

Tattle, now almost with tears of vexation, stamps his foot again on his next line of protest.

Valentine, enjoying the success of Scandal's ruse, smacks Tattle resoundingly on the back, which finally ruins his composure altogether, as Jeremy announces Mrs. Frail.

Tattle is now in a frenzy and makes for the door with little mincing steps (his heels are too high, probably).

Valentine, with huge enjoyment of the situation, seizes Tattle by the arm.

Tattle, flustered and in a shrill whisper, with eyes darting round the room: "Is there not a back way?"

Valentine's next line, with a struggle not to laugh, and with mock seriousness.

Tattle releases himself from Valentine's grip and rushes over to Scandal, who has been watching it all with malicious enjoyment, and his next speech pours out with a burst of tears.

Valentine from behind Tattle's back signals to Scandal the hint "he'll yield to any terms."

Tattle, wringing his hands, "Any, any terms."

Scandal, smiling at Valentine, delivers his ultimatum and Tattle moans, " 'Tis very hard," on which they all hear Mrs. Frail on the stairs outside saying (off) something to the effect of "This way, fellow?" to the servant,

88

instead of entering the scene as directed in the book. This gives time for Tattle's complete loss of control on "O unfortunate! she's come already—will you have patience till another time? I'll double the number," and as Scandal says: "Well, on that condition, take heed you don't fail me," Tattle dives behind him to get as far away from Mrs. Frail as possible.

MRS. FRAIL: I shall get a fine reputation by coming to see fellows in a morning. Scandal, you devil, are you here too? Oh, Mr. Tattle, everything is safe with you, we know.

SCANDAL: Tattle!

TATTLE: Mum!—O madam, you do me too much honour.

VALENTINE: Well, lady galloper, how does Angelica?

MRS. FRAIL: Angelica? Manners!

VALENTINE: What, you will allow an absent lover——

MRS. FRAIL: No, I'll allow a lover present with his mistress to be particular; but otherwise I think his passion ought to give place to his manners.

VALENTINE: But what if he has more passion than manners?

MRS. FRAIL: Then let him marry and reform.

VALENTINE: Marriage, indeed, may qualify the fury of his passion, but it very rarely mends a man's manners.

MRS. FRAIL: You are the most mistaken in the world; there is no creature perfectly civil but a husband. For in a little time he grows only rude to his wife, and that is the highest good breeding, for it begets his civility to other people. Well, and what will you give me now? Come, I must have something.

VALENTINE: Step into the next room—and I'll give you something.

SCANDAL: Ay, we'll all give you something.

MRS. FRAIL: Well, what will you all give me?

VALENTINE: Mine's a secret.

MRS. FRAIL: I thought you would give me something that would be a trouble to you to keep.

VALENTINE: And Scandal shall give you a good name.

MRS. FRAIL: That's more than he has for himself. And what will you give me, Mr. Tattle?

TATTLE: I? My soul, madam.

MRS. FRAIL: Pooh, no, I thank you. I have enough to do to take care of my own. Well; but I'll come and see you one of these mornings. I hear you have a great many pictures.

TATTLE: I have a pretty good collection at your service —some originals.

SCANDAL: Hang him, he has nothing but the Seasons and the Twelve Cæsars—paltry copies; and the Five Senses—as ill represented as they are in himself; and he himself is the only original you will see there.

MRS. FRAIL: Ay, but I hear he has a closet of beauties.

SCANDAL: Yes, all that have done him favours, if you will believe him.

MRS. FRAIL: Ay, let me see those, Mr. Tattle.

TATTLE: Oh, madam, those are sacred to love and contemplation. No man but the painter and myself was ever blest with the sight.

MRS. FRAIL: Well, but a woman—

TATTLE: Nor woman, till she consented to have her picture there too—for then she's obliged to keep the secret.

SCANDAL: No, no; come to me if you'd see pictures.

MRS. FRAIL: You?

SCANDAL: Yes, faith, I can show you your own picture, and most of your acquaintance to the life, and as like as at Kneller's.

MRS. FRAIL: O lying creature! Valentine, does not he lie? I can't believe a word he says.

VALENTINE: No, indeed, he speaks truth now; for as Tattle has pictures of all that have granted him favours, he has the pictures of all that have refused him; if satires, descriptions, characters, and lampoons are pictures.

Mrs. Frail is as gay, as shallow and as impudent as one can make her, equipped with a fan and perhaps a long stick and with her nodding fontage perched on her high-dressed wig. She has no moral standards of any kind, so that nothing she says should be shocking in itself as she is unaware of any other mode of life. She makes a deep curtsey as she boldly looks the men in the eye and dares them to suggest that her reputation could not be worse than it is! "Scandal, you devil, are you here too?" briskly rapping him with her closed fan. Then surprised at Mr. Tattle, whom she espies trying to hide behind Scandal. "Oh, Mr. Tattle—everything is safe with you, we know," with gay sarcasm.

As she seats herself with feminine fuss and billowing out of skirts and tossing of her head-dress, Scandal whispers with a provocative upward inflection: "Tattle!" as much as to say "We're watching you—we know better." And Tattle in an agony of embarrassment pleads: "Mum" (or, Be quiet!) in his ear, then tries to recover himself, with little success, on "O Madam, you do me too much honour," with one eye on Scandal. Valentine has taken Mrs. Frail's stick and as he puts it against the wall looks over his shoulder at Tattle with amusement. He then comes down to Mrs. Frail and the next passage is just conscious, graceful play of wit between them: gay and arch and artificial on her part, frankly enjoying her power of repartee and with sparkle all over her, nodding fontage, eyes, fingers, fan and toes alert and merry. If the actress merely enjoys the fun of the dialogue here it is all that is necessary. She scents antagonism in Scandal and Valentine and her retorts are rather acid—but "What will you give me, Mr. Tattle?" is sheer mischief —she knows she has him in her power. His reply is affected because the other two men are enjoying his discomfiture. She is deliberately teasing him and his veiled retorts should be directly at her, and through it all the other two men appreciate the situation, knowing that he has been admitted to her favours. Her attention is then caught by Scandal and she is deliberately co-quettish with him on "O lying creature! Valentine, does he not lie? I can't believe a word he says," with little glances under her eyelids and a provocative smile.

SCANDAL: Yes, mine are most in black and white;—and yet there are some set out in their true colours—both men and women. I can show you pride, folly, affectation, wantonness, inconstancy, covetousness, dis-simulation, malice, and ignorance—all in one piece. Then I can show you lying, foppery, vanity, cowardice, bragging, lechery, impotence, and ugliness in another piece; and yet one of these is a celebrated beauty, and t'other a professed beau. I have paintings, too, some pleasant enough.

MRS. FRAIL: Come, let's hear 'em.

SCANDAL: Why, I have a beau in a bagnio, cupping for a complexion, and sweating for a shape.

MRS. FRAIL: So.

SCANDAL: Then I have a lady burning brandy in a cellar with a hackney coachman.

MRS. FRAIL: O devil! Well, but that story is not true.

[*Re-enter* JEREMY

JEREMY: Sir, here's the steward again from your father.

VALENTINE: I'll come to him. Will you give me leave? I'll wait on you again presently.

MRS. FRAIL: No, I'll be gone. Come, who squires me

to the Exchange? I must call my sister Foresight there.

SCANDAL: I will: I have a mind to your sister.

MRS. FRAIL: Civil!

TATTLE: I will, because I have a *tendre* for your ladyship.

MRS. FRAIL: That's somewhat the better reason, to my opinion.

SCANDAL: Well, if Tattle entertains you, I have the better opportunity to engage your sister.

VALENTINE: Tell Angelica, I am about making hard conditions to come abroad, and be at liberty to see her.

SCANDAL: I'll give an account of you and your proceedings. If discretion be a sign of love, you are the most a lover of anybody that I know: you fancy that parting with your estate will help you to your mistress. In my mind he is a thoughtless adventurer,

Who hopes to purchase wealth by selling land,
Or win a mistress with a losing hand.   [*Exeunt*

Scandal's speech should be given with real sincerity and bitterness. The lines about "pride, folly, affectation" should be delivered straight at Mrs. Frail. She pretends not to apply them to herself and listens with amused, raised eyebrows. The following lines, "Lying, foppery, etc." he aims at Tattle, who bridles and looks annoyed at the implications. Mrs. Frail, greatly daring, encourages Scandal with "Come, let's hear 'em," and at Scandal's reference to Tattle as "a beau in a bagnio cupping for a complexion" she is wholeheartedly malicious

94

in her enjoyment and laughs "So!" behind her fan, gazing at the discomforted Tattle over it. When Scandal rounds on her with his next remark she is completely taken aback, and her "O devil—Well, but that story is not true" is suddenly quite sincere and outraged, and should be rapped out with real anger. This sudden simplicity has the comic effect of making her tacitly admit all Scandal's other innuendoes. She denies the very worst and thereby seems to acknowledge the others.

When the manservant enters Mrs. Frail at once goes back to her gay predatory behaviour as she rises to her feet and says "Who'll squire me to the Exchange?" with fan upheld, and the other arm out as if inviting anyone to take it. Scandal does so, with his malicious remark: "I will, I have a mind to your sister." Mrs. Frail tears her arm from his and raps him with her fan on her outraged "Civil!" Tattle pushes Scandal aside and takes her arm delicately on his line, while she throws her retort over her shoulder to Scandal and sails out.

There! That should be enough to keep you busy!

Yours ever,

ATHENE.

6th May 1940.

DEAR ATHENE,
Keep us busy indeed! That Sunday evening went on into Monday morning, and it was four o'clock before we finally stopped out of sheer fatigue. There

95

must have been something about wearing the costumes which encouraged my young friends to let themselves go, for the rehearsal was a great success. We began by reading your two last letters aloud and then we tackled the scene from *Love for Love*. My pupils worked hard and were quick to take production, and the scene came alive at once. Of course, technically they are still far from perfect. They aren't able to speak those long, artificial sentences with that mixture of precision and nonchalance which they require, nor (in spite of the costumes) have they succeeded yet in disguising their very twentieth-century bodies. But the intention and the sensitivity are there, and I really think that these are actors in the making.

William tells me that he has now decided to leave the bank and go on the professional stage. With the careless impetuosity of youth he has already given in his notice and will, I gather, be one of the unemployed next month. As I feel responsible for this decision of his I am organizing the production of a play under the auspices of his Bank Amateur Dramatic Society—we shall *not* do *Anatol* this time, I think!—to which I intend to invite some managers of repertory companies. In the meantime we are working at voice production, diction and movement—not that I expect these lessons to show much result in a month, but the discipline will be good for William. He is a glutton for work now, and whatever can be learnt in the time he will learn, I am sure. I'm afraid he still thinks that training to be an actor is only a matter of concentration; he doesn't realize that, for physical reasons alone, it takes two years to train a voice and to learn to control one's diaphragm and that, howeve. good one may be at football or cricket, one's movements are not therefore necessarily perfect for the stage. But no doubt he will find this out in time. He's a true optimist, which is probably a good thing. I can't say I feel very confident myself of securing him a job on the strength of one amateur performance, but such things have been done before and we may succeed this time. In any case he has taken his decision and it's clear he means to abide by it.

No doubt I ought now to start filling him up with good advice, but in my experience theoretical advice is difficult to give to any young actor. Each one of us experiences life in such a personal and individual manner on the stage that to be forewarned is not necessarily to be forearmed. Too much good advice may rob one of one's self-confidence and initiative. I think perhaps the best advice I had was from a friend who wrote: "You tell me you are going on the stage? Well, there are only two things to be said to that: (1) For God's sake don't; and (2) if you must, go ahead and God bless you."

I have been saying this in one form or another to William for the past twelve months. Like all actors— and I know you agree with me in this—I have done my best to dissuade him from going on the stage. But I can't help respecting his obstinate determination to disregard this excellent advice and now that I am sure he is wholehearted in his decision I should like to do all I can to help him.

So I wondered if you would very kindly add your own encouragement—and, if you like, dissuasion—to mine, and write him one more letter, containing any sort of advice that you think might be useful to him now that he is to be a professional actor. Your previous letters have naturally dealt with rather technical matters; possibly you would care to write a little now about the more personal aspects of our job. I leave it to you. If you could spare the time I know that William would have much to thank you for.

Yours ever,

Stephen.

16th May 1940.

Dear Stephen,

I was a little sad to hear that our happy and confident young amateur is to join the ranks of the disillusioned professional actors. He is marrying his mistress, as it were, and what has up till now been simply delight in the expression of his love for her will turn into staid responsibility and monotony with all the other cares attendant upon married life. He must now expect to give to acting all the devotion, duty and sacrifice that a husband ought to give his wife—and as we know this is a serious matter. I believe in marriage, and in the profession of acting too, and I know that neither should be embarked upon lightly. And what demands they make on one!

Has William courage and good health? These are as important, in my opinion, as talent. Does he aspire to be a power in the theatre, a leader, and, more vulgarly, a star? Then let him be prepared to devote his entire energies, thoughts and interest to his job. He must breathe, eat and dream the theatre: I have never known a successful actor do less. This will limit him as a person and as a citizen. He must of necessity be an egoist, and will probably become a bore. He must give up a wider life and concentrate on his job. Possibly he will find all this worth while.

If, however, he only aspires to filling some smaller place in the world of the theatre and has less ambition and a humbler view of his contribution to his art he may well lead a fairly normal life, with some leisure to cultivate interests outside his work, and perhaps a reasonable chance of making his living. But, whatever place he fills, courage will be a necessity to him. Remind him that our battles are never won. If we imagine we have made a success, we have then to repeat it and repeat it, right up to the end of our careers. We can never rest on our oars, for the stream is much too fast. Continual effort is required, and one must have a stout heart to withstand the strain.

Tell him that he must always regard any salary he earns as being only half its apparent value—and then to remember the income tax—for, with out-of-work periods, long rehearsals and short runs an actor's working year is often not much more than twenty-six weeks long. Warn him also of the difference between the enthusiasm of his friends at the one or two yearly performances to full houses which he now enjoys, and the instant criticism of these same friends when he appears on the professional stage and has to please them commercially at higher prices and in competition with other theatres. He will be surprised! The relations who will pay five shillings once a year to see dear William in a revival of a nearly forgotten play and tell him he is much better than Irving in the part will think twice about paying ordinary theatre prices to see him in a new play at the Globe, and then won't hesitate to condemn everything in the production, including himself.

One great compensation he will find in the theatre and that is the unique comradeship which it affords to its members. No other job brings one into quite the same relation with one's fellow-workers. It is sometimes, perhaps, a superficial relationship; it is tinged with jealousies and animosities. But it has one saving grace: it brings one closely together in success and failure, it makes each person dependent on the other's efforts, and I think you will agree with me that the bond between people who have both suffered and succeeded together is a very strong one as a rule.

I experienced this very acutely on my return from a world tour. I had left kind strangers and was returning to family and personal friends. But added to this was the knowledge that my first walk down Shaftesbury Avenue would bring me the sight of some fellow-actor or actress, the joy of meeting whom would spring from the bonds of work we had shared, of hopes we had enjoyed together and of failures we had mutually borne. It is a rare tie, and very precious once one is aware of it. Many actors, I believe, enjoy it quite unconsciously; so point it out to William as one of the compensations of the precarious and exacting job he has embarked upon.

Give him my best wishes, not for success but for achievement. He will mix the two up in his mind for some years, but if he is an artist he will distinguish between them in time. And beg him from me to keep uppermost in his mind that sense of proportion which is so essential to comedy—and to life.

Yours ever,

ATHENE.

31st May 1940.

DEAR ATHENE,

I am sad too. In fact this is altogether a melancholy occasion, partly because I have enjoyed this correspondence very much and it is now drawing to a close, and partly too because there is always something a little sad to an observer in the courageous recklessness of youth. "*Si la jeunesse savait* . . . !"

Your last letter, wise and kind-hearted as it is, contains the best advice our young friend will probably ever get, and after he has read it he will be better prepared than most young actors or actresses have the luck to be for the struggle of life in the theatre. But still, I cannot help feeling sad at seeing him off on his journey. I know too well how much disappointment lies in store for him, even though it may be more than redeemed by the colour and magic of the stage.

I don't think I have anything to add for William's benefit to what you have said; you seem to have touched on all the important questions which he will sooner or later be called upon to solve, not the least of which is this business of whether one is to be a great, an utterly self-absorbed actor, or whether one can allow oneself to lead a fairly normal life, with the wider spheres of interest which can develop one's personality beyond mere egoism. It is a problem which has vexed me considerably. I cannot feel, somehow, that acting could ever be my sole ambition. Although I desire the wealth and success, and the satisfaction of achievement which there is in acting, I resent the narrowing down of one's spiritual and mental development which seems to be the price of these things. And as I hate doing things half-heartedly I have often decided to leave the stage and earn my living in some other way rather than endure this perpetual struggle between self-development and self-advertisement. I think the only thing that has prevented me from doing so has been the ever-increasing fascination which the art of the theatre exercises over me, and the sheer ambition of achieving perfection in this art—a hopeless ambition, of course, since we all know that no true artist ever believes he has achieved perfection. Then, too, the more I learn of the theatre the more I love it and the people who work in it; so the struggle in my mind is further complicated by considerations of loyalty and friendship. For I think that what you say about the comradeship of the theatre is very true: it is a unique one and a very precious compensation for the difficulties we encounter.

I have been wondering what to give William as a souvenir of this great decision he has taken. On such occasions one is usually given a book on costume or make-up, or perhaps a more welcome fiver. Sometimes one is given nothing but advice. I think I shall have all your letters bound into a book for him, together with my replies, in order to preserve the sequence of the thought. The wisdom which you have poured into these letters is sure to be of use to him—a kind of friendly iron railing to guide him through the dark nights of his artistic soul. The clarity of your thought and the soundness of your principles of the theatre ought to save him from those wretched bouts of artiness which seem to attack most young actors at one time or another. And the experience you have conveyed to him should enable him to start several laps ahead of his rivals; because I believe that if he lives to be a hundred he will never find out more about comedy acting than you have put into this correspondence.

I should like to thank you for the help you have given him. But I am sure that no words of mine will please you as much as William's success when it comes. So I shall say no more, but send William cheerfully out into the world of the theatre with this volume of your precepts in his hand.

Yours ever,

STEPHEN.

FANS, TRAINS AND STAYS

A Series of Letters on the Art of "Period Acting"

(Impressed with the superiority of English to American actors in the technique of so-called "period acting," the editors of *Theatre Arts* asked Miss Seyler for her theories on the actor's interpretation of plays of other times, and on the adaptation of a particular period. She responded in the following series of letters written during her tour of England in *Lady Windermere's Fan*.)

Manchester

I should like to oblige, but Oh! my first reaction is that so much too much is written and said that is only chatter in print and not of any value. I've really no idea why British actors play period pieces better than Americans. What can one say? That the continuity of tradition in this country tends increasingly to influence us? That we have an innate conservatism in this island that preserves a cultural line of thought? (What a phrase!)

I suppose it is true that a certain crispness of speech and a precision of movement—an elegance of gesture and an assumption of artificiality—come more easily to an English-bred actor than to one who is used to more loose slang, to easy drawl in speech and more freedom of manners. We have kept a clipped, reserved tradition of speech and manners through our aristocracy and public-school system, which has to be sacrificed in a land of more progressive democratic ideas. And without saying that one is better than the other it may help us over the smaller issues of period acting.

I've been coaching our new Lady Windermere in how to use a fan in the nineteenth-century way, and someone (for John Gielgud's New York production of *Love for Love*) in how to use one in the seventeenth-century manner! . . .

Adelphi Hotel, Liverpool

Why should one set up to know anything about the use of the fan in any historical period? I very certainly have never read any descriptions, nor do contemporary pictures give more than an indication here and there. I suppose one bases any guesses one may make about these periods on what one knows of their customs and background and of the spirit of their times.

In England we are never far from history. All day long we are in touch with historic customs, with buildings and traditions still surviving from bygone centuries. Think of the civic functions, of the openings of Parliament, of our coronations and royal occasions which must foster in us almost unconsciously a sense of continuity in formal manners. One cannot enter any art gallery or any of the great houses open to the public without constant reminders of the fashions and particular attributes of different centuries, shown in contemporary portraits and period furniture.

For instance, the use of a fan must have indicated and reflected the same attitude towards life as shows in the style of the hair-dressing, of the clothes and of the dances of any given age. The late seventeenth-century women wore a mass of shaking curls, bared their bosoms and evidently had flung themselves out of Puritanism with a gay vengeance. So what more reasonable than to suggest in a Restoration play that one should flirt one's fan and flutter it gaily around one's curls, or gaze archly over it?

In the next century one would gather from its more formal and exaggerated character, from the grace and dignity of the minuet and the pomp of the hair styles, together with the idiosyncrasies of the huge hats, that fans were also larger in proportions and, as we know, exquisitely painted. So perhaps a more measured movement in their use—and a pose held with them at arm's length, to display them to the fullest advantage—would be correct.

Victorian influences substituted demure bonnets for Gainsborough hats, and dresses which emphasized delicacy and weakness in women's behavior. What more suitable than to use a fan to ward off difficulties (or over-heat), with a modest stirring of the air around one's temples and a discreet shadowing of one's face from the bold gaze of one's partner?

At least so I see it! And if this is not strictly what the real ladies of those days did with a fan, at least it will give an audience the spirit of the times and will be in keeping with the manner of the plays of these periods—which is what an actress sets out to do.

Leeds

You ask about the "period acting" of the French in comedy and whether they are similar to us or different in their "period" traditions, and I have to confess that I have never seen a Moliere comedy done by the Comedie Francaise, and in fact have actually seen only two productions from that theatre: once in 1914, I think— *Hernani*—and once last time they were over here— *Ruy Blas*.

Each time I regret to say it seemed to me that tradition weighed so heavily on the shoulders of the actors that behind I could see a long line of identical arms making the same gestures on the same cues, with the same inflections and pauses, as one sees oneself repeated unendingly in mirrors that face each other. The repetition was, I am sure, of some originally fine inspiration, but to me only the mechanics were left. I had the impression that the technique of tragic acting (and perhaps I should have felt the same about comedy) was far more detailed, cut and dried, and inexorable than our own. Perhaps this comes from their having had for

108

so long a static academy of acting where technique was perfected and then—I was going to say pickled—at least preserved intact from a former age.

In England we have no such museum of acting—alas! I think much of value has been lost for this reason, but it has left us a little more elastic and varied in our attack—witness Mr. Gielgud's season of repertory in 1945, when his Hamlet had quite a new angle, from which we could see what was intrinsic in his performance ever since he first played it many years ago, but now newly informed and considered.

When one compares Sir Laurence Olivier's performance of the same part one sees at once that there is no common tradition of tragic acting such as I felt I recognized at the Comedie Francaise, and in a lesser degree I expect this to be true of classic comedy. The precision and intellectual tidiness of the French mind is so unlike our own that their comedy acting may well be much more formalized and clearly defined than ours, for national characteristics I believe are clearly shown in the art of different countries.

The wealth of natural gesture that the French use in acting (as in their normal life) and the greater mobility of their facial expression must give more force to their comedic expression. Our tradition is much more in understatement and oblique methods, and in comedy may seem to have less emphasis. But surely in pantomime and expressive by-play the French must be as superb in classic comedy as they certainly are in modern plays. . . .

About wearing period costume: The most important thing is not the dress one wears but what one wears underneath it, and in one's mind. That is to say, the best Edwardian creation put over a modern elastic belt, and worn by someone who crosses her legs and throws her chest in or stands with her weight on one hip, will never look in the least right. On the other hand, give me a pair of boned corsets high under the bust and to a point in front and laced tightly to the waist, and at least three full stiff petticoats, and I shall be able to wear a tablecloth and a lace antimacassar with a good suggestion of 1870.

But of course I must have the line of the train on the floor and remember to kick my skirt neatly ahead of me with my feet as I walk so as not to tread into it. I must hold my head erect and my back very straight, sit with one foot a trifle in front of the other on the floor, never lounge (even if one could in corsets), never put my hands on my hips but keep them neatly folded on my lap.

I am wearing a train at the moment of writing which is quite a yard long on the floor and incredibly heavy. How the modern young actress gets scared of this and says she can't move this way, or, if it is a shorter day-gown of light material, to catch it at arms length behind and quietly lift it as one walks. It needs quite a deal of practice to get a train properly to heel, if I may put it that way, with elegance and neatness.

Do you realize how different a shape one's corset makes one? The modern "girdle" gives a pear-shaped line behind, increases one's waist measurement and leaves one's bust to uplift or to constraint. When one puts on stays of the Victorian and Edwardian period, one's waist is two inches smaller, one's hips correspondingly bigger, and the line of the bosom is raised quite two inches again and neatly thrown into a shelf under one's chin when one sits down! So you can see how important it is to have one's shape the correct foundation for a dress to hang on.

I believe that in the sixteenth century, stays were not made of whalebones but wood, and that long stiff line in front on which the slender Elizabethan torso was molded gave women quite a different line again. I've never worn wooden corsets with an Elizabethan costume, but probably we would all look less like fancy dress and more like the originals if we did.

Shoes, of course, are of great importance in giving one the correct poise for a dress. Impossible to swim with tiny steps under a crinoline in modern high-heeled court shoes or wedge heels. One must have either flat sandals with ribbons crossed up the ankles or such low heels as to be nearly flat. The seventeenth century had square toes and perhaps one-and-a-half-inch heels, and not till the eighteenth century did one have higher ones, and even so these were "Louis-shaped" and did not tilt one forward as the modern shoe does. One's walk and stance are quite determined by one's shoes, as one can see when one changes from brogues to evening slippers nowadays.

So how important they must be to an actress in assuming period dress!

I've rather left men out of this discussion, but I am not altogether popular with younger actors when directing them in an 1890 play and forbidding them to put their hands in their pockets! But perhaps I had better leave them to one of their own sex for instruction as to how to negotiate a top hat, a cane and a four-inch collar!

All we want in Kenilworth at the moment is a mackintosh and snow boots—how simple to wear! . . .

The Grand Hotel, Plymouth

You asked me about producers and production, or as you say directors and directing? I've never worked with John Gielgud, but having come into one of his nineteenth-century productions (*Lady Windermere's Fan*) and seen his other Wilde plays I guess that he stresses mainly style in directing any period play. Now, I find that the question of keeping the balance between the artificiality of the period and the true characterization and humanity beneath the surface wit is as debatable a subject as the age-long discussion of "sound versus sense" in speaking Shakespeare! There must be a happy means whereby one can joy in the form and fantastication of the dialogue and yet bring out all the meaning of the lines. I am sure myself that the modern throw-away method is no use to dramatists such as Wycherley or

Congreve and that the fullest value must be given to every single word. But in doing this one is apt to use forced inflections and unreal tones—it is just the trick of accomplishing the one and avoiding the other extreme that constitutes the charm and difficulty of speaking period plays. A fastidious ear and a simple heart should be the successful combination.

What about setting? Stylized or naturalistic? I believe I can play Restoration drama in either, happily, and have indeed done so. Nigel Playfair favored the first kind of approach, and I remember a delightful set in which we did *Marriage à la Mode* where he had a permanent Renaissance bridge across the back of the stage with two flights of steps leading up to it each side. This enabled him to invent my entrances and exits as Melantha, the ridiculous Frenchified lady—up one flight, across the bridge and down the other side each time—and as I had bunches of curls hanging each side of a huge hair arrangement, they bobbed and flew about with each step up and down and made a perfect visual gay joke of one's appearance. That I consider true and imaginative production, for it used legitimately a device to emphasize the peculiarities and modes of the time.

A great deal of space and room to move in is a boon to an actress in a seventeenth-century play, for breadth of gesture is essential. A stage cluttered up with furniture is probably quite wrong in that century. The scenes are obviously intended to be played very often with sweeping movements and on the feet more than in the modern "sits settee left" type of acting.

I like a lot of light for artificial comedy—and footlights—and every gay help of music and color to add to the theatricality of these old plays. No subtle shadows or half-lights, no modernistic crudities; preferable, for me, should a setting be "pretty," with any coarseness in the text softened by a charming background.

I do not believe that the old plays—essentially forthright and straightforward in essence as they are—need or, indeed, allow of fantastication or of distortion in their setting. Everything about the production should be as sparkling and lucid as possible. With which few notes I leave the field clear to any of our more adventurous producers who care to challenge my theories in practice.

1947